1990

The Teaching of Et[...]

Ethical Dilemmas and the Education of Policymakers

Joel L. Fleishman
Bruce L. Payne

INSTITUTE OF
SOCIETY, ETHICS AND
THE LIFE
SCIENCES THE
HASTINGS
CENTER

The Hastings Center
Institute of Society, Ethics and the Life Sciences
360 Broadway
Hastings-on-Hudson, New York 10706

Library of Congress Cataloging in Publication Data

Fleishman, Joel L
    Ethical dilemmas and the education of policymakers.
    (The Teaching of ethics ; 7)
    Bibliography: p.
    1. Political ethics—Study and teaching (Higher)—
United States. I. Payne, Bruce L., joint author.
II. Title. III. Series: Teaching of ethics ; 7.
JA79.F62   172'.07'1173   80–10230
ISBN 0–916558–05–3

Printed in the United States of America

Contents

FOREWORD

A concern for the ethical instruction and formation of students has always been a part of American higher education. Yet that concern has by no means been uniform or free of controversy. The centrality of moral philosophy in the undergraduate curriculum during the mid-nineteenth century gave way later during that century to the first signs of increasing specialization of the disciplines. By the middle of the twentieth century, instruction in ethics had, by and large, become confined almost exclusively to departments of philosophy and religion. Efforts to introduce ethics teaching in the professional schools and elsewhere in the university often met with indifference or outright hostility.

The past decade has seen a remarkable resurgence of interest in the teaching of ethics at both the undergraduate and professional school levels. Beginning in 1977, The Hastings Center, with the support of the Rockefeller Brothers Fund and the Carnegie Corporation of New York, undertook a systematic study of the teaching of ethics in American higher education. Our concern focused on the extent and quality of that teaching, and on the main possibilities and problems posed by widespread efforts to find a more central and significant role for ethics in the curriculum.

As part of that project, a number of papers, studies, and monographs were commissioned. Moreover, in an attempt to gain some degree of consensus, the authors of those studies worked together as a group for a period of two years. The study presented here represents one outcome of the project. We hope and believe it will be helpful for those concerned to advance and deepen the teaching of ethics in higher education.

Daniel Callahan   Sissela Bok
Project Co-Directors
The Hastings Center
Project on the Teaching of Ethics

v

About the Authors

Joel L. Fleishman

Joel L. Fleishman is Professor of Law and Public Policy, as well as Director of the Institute of Policy Sciences and Public Affairs at Duke University. He received his A.B., M.A. and J.D. from the University of North Carolina at Chapel Hill, and his Master of Laws from Yale. He has written numerous articles on political campaign finance reform and political ethics, and has served as chairman of the Harvard Faculty Study Group on the Moral Obligations of Public Officials. He is at present serving as President of the Association for Public Policy Analysis and Management.

Bruce L. Payne

Bruce L. Payne is a lecturer in policy sciences and public affairs at Duke University where he teaches courses in ethics and policymaking. He is at work on a study of the religious and political ideas of Thomas Szasz, and on an investigation of ideas of quality and democracy in relation to public support for the arts.

Acknowledgments

Several individuals and institutions have provided generous help in the preparation of this paper. We are especially grateful to the Rockefeller Foundation and to the Institute of Politics at Harvard University's John F. Kennedy School of Government for their support of the Faculty Study Group on the Moral Obligations of Public Officials. The continuing discussions among our colleagues in that Faculty Study Group over a two-year period have been invaluable. In addition, the Rockefeller Foundation earlier made possible a series of faculty seminars at Duke University on the same subject. We are eager to acknowledge our gratitude to the participants in both series of discussions, many of whose insights we have included here.

The lively discussions of The Hastings Center Project on the Teaching of Ethics, supported by a grant from The Carnegie Corporation, have also been extremely helpful. To Sissela Bok and Daniel Callahan, who have guided this project, we own special thanks for counsel and encouragement. We are also greatly indebted to Professors Don K. Price of Harvard, Dennis Thompson of Princeton, and Charles Wolf of the Rand Graduate Institute for their very thoughtful responses to an earlier draft of this paper, and to several other participants in The Hastings Center Project who have taken the time to comment on our ideas.

We are especially fortunate in having been able to work closely with Professor David Price, our colleague in the Duke Institute. Our debt to his clear thinking about the problems of ethics and policymaking is a large one.

Introduction

The proud claim that ours is a government of laws should not be allowed to obscure the fact that it is also a government of men and women. Our officials have considerable discretion; to cope successfully with complex problems, or to increase governmental effectiveness, even more may be required. What assurances do we have that our officials will be guided, and indeed limited, by the wishes and needs of citizens? What hopes may we entertain of improving the quality of decisions made on our behalf?

While the concern for ethical governance can be traced almost as far back in history as the written word itself, two kinds of considerations have given this problem a special urgency in recent years. The introduction of highly sophisticated analytic techniques has seemed to weaken the influence of moral concern by encouraging a narrowly practical and technological view of policymaking. At the same time, repeated instances of conflict of interest, lying, official lawbreaking, and other abuses of power at high levels of the government have given the impression that American public ethics are in a state of crisis or decay.

We are convinced that the events of the past decade and a half do not manifest any decline in official morality. On the contrary, standards appear to be higher than ever, even if many shortcomings still remain. But there *are* shortcomings, and in our polity there is no reason to tolerate them.

For the long-term health of our democracy, it is urgent that policymakers become more moral, and that fundamental social choices be more thoughtfully made. Levels of deception and corruption that once seemed tolerable now threaten to undermine confidence in government, a condition made all the more serious by the complexity and difficulty of the tasks of distribution, redistribution, and regulation which government has assumed. To make matters worse, as the stakes have gotten higher, the quality of public debate on many important issues has declined.

While formal education is not the most important influence on an individual's moral behavior, we firmly believe the education of public officials can increase the likelihood that they will act more ethically—that they will be more sensitive to the responsibilities they have undertaken, more alert to the consequences of their acts, more careful in observing the laws and rules that regulate conduct. Some kinds of academic preparation, in policy curricula as well as elsewhere, already go part of the way toward meeting these needs. But in our opinion, much more can and should be done.

In this paper we mean to describe some of what is being done now and to make recommendations about additional courses and other efforts that will improve teaching in the field. Accordingly, our paper begins with a description of the courses currently being offered in the field of ethics and policy, and with a discussion of some of the reasons that serious work in this area has been rare. Recommendations about curricular changes and faculty training and development comprise a second part. The third section, by far the longest, is designed to set out in some detail the range and variety of ethical problems policymakers actually face.

I. Ethics in the Policy Curriculum

Ethical issues have only rarely been at the center of education for public service or of the study of government. The newly created schools and programs in public policy do show an increasing interest in ethical problems generally; a certain rather narrow range of ethical concerns has always played a minor role in the study of public administration, and political science departments have maintained some continuing interest in normative theory. Yet across the whole landscape of these studies the explicit consideration of ethical questions has for the most part been peripheral.

The predominance of scientific models for the study of politics is one reason for the relative weakness of ethics in the various institutions and departments. Political theory and moral reasoning have seemed unscientifically "soft," fatally infected with emotion or ideology. Other reasons, however, may be at least as important. The conceptual difficulties described in the third part of the paper have posed formidable barriers to serious ethical analysis, and so too have the inadequacies of traditional approaches to the teaching of ethics.

A. Ethics and the Study of Public Policy

It has taken only a little more than a decade for the field of public policy analysis to establish itself firmly as an academic enterprise. Graduate schools of public policy have been organized at a number of major universities, while many political science departments and several graduate schools and programs in public administration offer policy concentrations within their curricula. A substantial portion of the students receiving graduate degrees in policy are getting other advanced degrees, in law or the social sciences or, occasionally, medicine. The developing programs in policy have emphasized training in microeconomic analysis, statistical and computer techniques, and organizational theory. Growing out of operations research and systems analysis, the policy schools owe some of their impetus to the vigorous attempts in the early 1960s to reform and rationalize decisionmaking in the Department of Defense, and later in the federal government as a whole. The techniques of policy analysis are thus not the property of a single discipline. What distinguishes the policy programs is rather their emphasis on problem solving and applied knowledge, and their willingness to draw analytic techniques from many disciplines.

What is the current shape of teaching about ethics in the fields of public policy and administration? The short answer is that, in fewer than half of the programs surveyed, some coursework is offered.[1] In fewer than a quarter of the programs are semester-long courses required by the curriculum. Responses to our questionnaire indicate some substantial interest in expanding the number of courses taught, but it is clear that in many of these programs there is considerable faculty resistance to undertaking any substantial study of ethics and public policy, either because ethics courses are thought to be necessarily "soft," or because for each ethics course added, some other course, thought to be more important, would have to be omitted.

Among the courses that are taught, the majority focus primarily on policy issues involving conflicting values. Some of these are limited fairly narrowly to "hard choices," to the difficult problems of making trade-offs between competing values, such as efficiency and equity in relation to social programs. Others have dealt largely with the "moral issues" of abortion, homosexuality, criminal punishment, human rights, and the morality of war. Theoretical perspectives are present in these courses to varying degrees, and the topic of distributive justice is a primary point of departure for many of the discussions of specific issues. Courses stressing the responsibilities of individual decisionmakers also exist in some numbers. Like other work in policy, they are largely oriented to particular cases. Many such courses are built around conflicts between procedural and substantive values, reflecting with varying degrees of comprehensiveness the concerns we describe below as dilemmas of responsibility.

A third category of courses are those in which the problems of normative ethics play a primary role. Democratic theory, ideals of liberty and justice, and utilitarianism are favorite topics. Most of them devote considerable time to the study of policy questions in which these topics figure prominently; some are best described as being concerned equally with principles and particular substantive issues. There are, in addition, a very few ethics courses that are theoretical in a different way, using philosophical or literary materials to challenge accepted modes of thinking or to offer alternative ways of conceiving problems.

Ethics courses have a variety of sources and histories. Some, like one at Harvard's Kennedy School, were developed partly in response to student misgivings about the possibility that amoral or antimoral expertise would shape the commitments of the program. Others seem to have emerged more from the prominence of official malfeasance in public life—Watergate, corporate bribery, and the like. Almost all of the courses owe a considerable debt to the deep moral convictions of specific individuals involved in teaching about policymaking. For the most part, existing courses manifest a serious concern with ethical questions on the part of some people in the policy field. Nowhere, however, do courses in which ethical issues are central make up as much as 10 percent of the curriculum, and it is probably fair to say that a substantial majority of policy students graduate with no formal training in the subject.[2]

Some faculty object to this characterization as unfair, arguing that ethics in fact pervades the study of policy generally, or that at least all of the substantive courses in public policy are shot through with ethical concerns. In a superficial sense, this is obviously true. The techniques of decision analysis, microeconomic analysis, and the like have a considerable normative bite. They favor rationality in decisionmaking, and they are aimed at promoting efficiency. Democratic values and notions of equity appear, at least as constraints, in most pieces of policy analysis.

Such objections miss the mark. Without focused curricular attention, the pervasiveness of values in policy studies and policy
analysis does not go very far in teaching students about ethical
analysis. Undoubtedly, there are professors who teach analytic
techniques or the substance of policy in ways that reveal relevant
normative questions and thereby offer students a chance to see
value complexities and to develop their own critical stances on
moral questions. By all accounts such teaching is rare, though we
would agree that when it is present it may do much to extend the
reach of courses more explicitly oriented to ethical analysis.

Some of those who claim that ethics is already part of the
curriculum, who assert that no special courses in ethics are
needed, are in fact making a certain kind of claim about the role
and the nature of ethical analysis. Believing that ethics is inher-
ently subjective, and often also that values are at bottom only
emotional affirmations, they regard ethical investigations and
analysis as fruitless. A more common objection to the enterprise
of ethics in policy analysis is one that would limit the relevance
of ethics to a narrowly utilitarian and democratic framework,
arguing that the values of importance to policymaking are com-
prehended in the predominant techniques of analysis. These objections have limited severely the role played by ethical reasoning
in policy analysis. They deserve further examination.

B. Obstacles

The early reformist zeal of the policy analysts who hoped in
the 1960s to change the way decisions are made in Washington
has now somewhat abated. At their most hopeful, many thought
that the application of such techniques as systems analysis and
program budgeting would make possible the comparison of costs
and benefits across the whole body of governmental choices. The
advent of computerization had made the most complicated calculations possible, and it was hoped that the necessary simplifi-
cations and quantifications could be done without substantial bias
and without the loss of essential information.

It is now widely conceded that effective monetary comparisons
are possible only between largely similar programs and policies,
that comparisons of dollars spent on dams or pollution abatement

with dollars spent on weapons systems cannot be made in any way that clearly guides decisionmakers in choosing between them.[3] Yet the hope remains that benefit-cost analysis can provide an adequate paradigm for thinking about choices between programs of all shapes and sizes.

The analysis of benefits and costs is a guide to economic efficiency, and even its most enthusiastic partisans admit that it needs to be supplemented by judgments about equity. But some would argue that efficiency and equity are ethics enough. A recent, influential introductory text in policy analysis, for example, sets forth a conceptual scheme that amalgamates all the possible legitimate aims of government intervention in the allocation process to these two goals.[4] The position that has been developed by those policy analysts, and they are primarily economists, who have been most enthusiastic about benefit-cost analysis is not so much opposed to making value judgments as it is to the utility or appropriateness of ethical or philosophical argument. They urge that decisionmakers focus their analytic techniques on a particular social welfare function, and that they base their normative judgments chiefly on the models of welfare economics and on the results of "the established decision process of society."[5]

Those who take this position see the techniques of policy analysis as the appropriate means for coping with ethical questions. In our view this is mistaken. The problems we describe in subsequent parts of this paper can undoubtedly be translated into the language of this sort of analysis, but it seems to us that the translation will more likely obscure than clarify the important moral dimensions of the choices decisionmakers face. Nor does this perspective provide any independent basis for critical thinking about the principle of efficiency itself, or about the adequacy of the social decision process. That the language of economics is ethically inadequate does not, however, mean that it should be dismissed or replaced by more traditional forms of ethical analysis. Thinking clearly about moral implications of choices requires a clear understanding of the incidence of those costs and benefits amenable to measurement or to techniques of estimation. A large part of the spectrum of the things and conditions men value can be well illuminated by economic analysis.

If many economists are uninterested in expanding the field of ethics and policy because of confidence in their own normative frameworks, a considerable number of political scientists have similar reservations for quite opposite reasons. Philosophic positivism and the conviction that value judgments are emotive and not cognitive statements were part of the orthodoxy of behavioralism, that most successful of modern movements for the "scientific" study of politics. Political scientists holding these views have tended to argue that no ethical judgment about policy can rationally be made. A proper response to this view can only be a general defense of ethics, something hardly to be attempted here. A few of its implications nevertheless deserve comment.

One of the perhaps illegitimate attractions of the emotive theory of ethics was that it seemed to link ethical discussions with emotionalism. The factual investigations of scientists thus seemed to broaden the (good) area of reason in human affairs while ethical debate appeared to expand the (bad) realm of fervor and fanaticism.[6] Inconsistencies owing to value judgments smuggled in under the cloak of analysis are almost inevitable when positivists try to talk about anything important, but our concern in citing this rather widely held view is with the peculiar and mistaken notion it embodies of the appropriate response to emotion. The implicit presumption is that people who disagree about values can ultimately only come to blows,[7] and that the proper response to the passions roused by morality is, in psychological terms, repression. Such a view is consonant with the preference for consensual values which prevails among the positivists of the political science profession; the dominant values of the society, reinforced by its accepted political processes, can offer a solid basis for the maintenance of the political process the positivists wish to study. But as a response to passionate disagreement, it is inadequate. A refusal to debate important normative questions sometimes raises the pitch of fervor, while full and open debate about them may lead to compromise, or at least to the acceptance by dissident groups and individuals of unfavorable verdicts reached after a fair hearing of their views. Moreover, when disagreement is ignored or fair hearing denied, the rise in moral fervor may in fact destroy consensus. Then, there may be no settled norms to fall back on, and even positivists may be forced to agree to moral debate, if by that time the possibility has not disappeared.

A third and more important basis of opposition to more extensive ethical debate is the position known as "incrementalism."
Since choices, on this view, are so complex, and since it is
impossible to array all the values, no adequate normative scheme
is available to rank-order the options a decisionmaker faces.
Moreover, the subjectivity of value judgments leaves a decision-
maker with no authorization for imposing any judgments other
than those of the community. The goodness of a policy depends
on agreement, and it is even said that "...it is not irrational for a
policymaker to defend a policy as good without being able to
specify what it is good for."[8] This formulation may perhaps serve
to underscore our position on the need for normative debate.
Incrementalism is, in general, a reasonable approach to making
decisions; but it should be accompanied by normative debate, a
debate in which policymakers have an important role to play. A
policy that cannot be defended as good for something cannot be
defended at all.

The incrementalist position was developed in reaction to programs of fundamental social change. It grew partly out of the
realization that while radical theories, and Marxism in particular,
could envision a new order, their predictive ability was inversely
proportional to their breadth of vision. Rational political change,
it was argued, could go only so far as a choice between more or
less predictable outcomes, making piecemeal reform the only
possible course for attaining the results actually desired. Such an
analysis is an important corrective to much moral argument.
Although it may be rational to hold a radical position that insists
on one value above all others, an ideology that demands allegiance both to comprehensive social change involving multiple
values and to particular and drastic means to their achievement is
likely to be logically indefensible.

The general tendency of incrementalism to disparage debate
and ethical investigation probably owes something to its ancestry.
If normative analysis is perceived to be principally the clash of
the great political systems, it may accordingly seem that ethics
has little to contribute to the solution of the day-to-day problems
of government. Our analysis of ethical dilemmas shows, we
hope, that there are in fact many levels at which debate is the
proper complement to the incremental processes of decision. And

it ought not be forgotten that there are times, especially those of crisis, in which some kinds of fundamental questions must be debated.

One other comment should perhaps be made in response to the incrementalist position. Changes may indeed be best made step by step, so that consequences can be partly foreseen, and so that corrections can be made in response to unpredicted events. But the pace of change, as well as its direction, must always be chosen. While incrementalism of some sort may be the only rational position to take with regard to some types of policymaking, the variety of available stances includes both militant and cautious incrementalists, and both reactionaries and progressives.

Economists committed to benefit-cost analysis, political scientists half-convinced by positivism, and incrementalists among students of policy from various backgrounds are the major, though not the only, sources of opposition to a strengthening of ethical analysis in the policy curriculum. Their objections are not frivolous, and raise questions worth pondering by the partisans of normative analysis. In the final analysis, however, they seem unpersuasive as arguments against a larger place in the education of policymakers for ethics instruction which now hardly exists at all.

A few more practical problems have also been obstacles to good work in ethics and public policy. Those knowledgeable about political theory or philosophical ethics have given considerable effort to ultimate questions about politics—allegiance, justice, revolution, and the like. The more usual ethical dilemmas of policymaking have been dealt with less frequently, and when they have been examined at all, it has often been by means of hypothetical cases rather than actual history. For these reasons and many others there has been a shortage of literature linking ethical concerns directly to policy problems. The lack has been especially acute in relation to the questions of responsibility that we treat in the third part of this paper. Nor have there been many scholars adequately trained in ethical reasoning who are also broadly knowledgeable about the problems faced by governmental decisionmakers. Yet having such people seems almost a prerequisite for maintaining communication with others involved in the study of policy.

II. Recommendations

Students in the policy programs are for the most part both ambitious and concerned. They expect to have careers as public decisionmakers, or as policy analysts or journalists, and a good many of them can reasonably hope to reach high levels in their chosen fields. Many of them are strongly motivated by a reformist impulse; they hope to have a part in better choices than the ones they know. Although undergraduate programs in policy are growing, most of the policy students are graduates. Their time is limited, and they are often impatient to be done with academic training. Courses in ethics can be highly effective with such students, only if they are taught in such a way that their relevance to policymaking is clear.

Our notions about what courses ought to be taught, about the objectives of those courses, and about who should teach in them, are responsive to the needs of these students as we perceive them. While well-taught courses about any portion of the subjects we describe below might be helpful to decisionmakers, careful curricular choices ought to reflect both a sense of what issues and problems are most important and an estimate of the subjects to which students are most likely to respond.

A. Courses

We believe that every student of public policy ought to have at least one course dealing with the ethical dilemmas of policymaking, a view underscored in the Report of The Hastings Center Project on the Teaching of Ethics in Higher Education.[9] Such problems seem simply too important to be ignored; and no amount of technical expertise or knowledge about the substance of policy will give students the perspectives and critical skills they will need to face these problems. Although ethical discussions may and should occur in other courses, a separate full semester course offers the only opportunity for extended consideration of ethical issues, and the only chance for any substantial attention to the relevance of systematic and reflective thought about ethics in relation to the problems of policymaking.

A required course should, we think, deal both with problems of the responsibilities of individual policymakers and with the larger questions of better and worse in policy choice. In such a course, the proper balance of theoretical writings and material about cases and issues is hard to judge with confidence—good teaching is always important, and we all tend to teach better the things we know well. Still, we doubt the wisdom of teaching such a course at a primarily abstract level. Helping students to recognize ethical dilemmas as they actually face policymakers is an essential part of the instructional task.

Additional courses in which ethical questions are central seem to us also a necessary part of any policy program that means to take ethical issues seriously. Such courses might be electives in which theoretical problems are central, or in which policy issues or dilemmas of responsibility predominate. They might, on the other hand, be courses in substantive policy areas, in which the ethical dimensions of the issues play an important role.

In order to make a serious claim on the time and effort of policy students, courses in ethics and policymaking should be part of the policy curriculum and taught by members of the policy faculty. These courses can and should be as rigorous as others in the program. It is imperative that such courses avoid indoctrination, a problem dealt with at length in the Report of The Hastings Center Project.[10] The assertion of claims of certainty or the exclusion of opposing views must be incompatible with serious ethics teaching and are sure to discredit the enterprise. There is no need, however, for faculty to camouflage their own views. The best teaching about ethics and politics, as about

much else, communicates a sense of the importance of the subject.

B. Objectives

Policymakers and policy analysts need to be able to recognize
quickly the many ethical dilemmas of their work. The development of this skill strikes us as the first goal of courses in ethics
and policy. Students need to know how complex and difficult
ethical problems are likely to be. They need to see that good
intentions are insufficient if unaccompanied by a clear understanding of the moral stakes involved in the choices policymakers
face.

Because of this fundamental aim, teaching about ethics and
policy will seldom succeed if it depends on prepackaged or hypothetical accounts of ethical dilemmas. The crucial task is to identify the ethical issues in the midst of all the complexity and moral
uncertainty of their historical contexts. In this connection, it may
be worth noting that those programs in which history already
plays an important role, in which analytic problems are illuminated by the consideration of earlier attempts to solve similar
problems, offer a strong supporting culture for work in ethics and
policymaking. Similarly, the development of an adequately complex understanding of ethical dilemmas is more readily achievable
in programs not dominated by a single analytic paradigm—programs where legal argument, organization theory, and sometimes
divergent political views supplement the perspectives of economic
analysis. This aim, and those outlined below, are among the five
goals set forth as imperative in the Report of The Hastings Center
Project on the Teaching of Ethics in Higher Education.[11]

Our second main objective in courses in ethics and policy is to
develop skills of ethical analysis. Skill is needed particularly in
the careful weighing, for logic and relevance and coherence, of
the sorts of normative argument policymakers face from contend-
ing parties. And skill is also needed for reasoning about the competing obligations decisionmakers undertake.

A third general aim might be described as raising the level of
moral anxiety, or as stimulating the moral imaginations of stu-

dents. Beyond the ability to recognize and to analyze moral problems, students need to encounter their own moral feelings and their personal moral judgments. Sorting out the contradictions of one's own views may be an uncomfortable process, but that kind of personal moral involvement can be a spur to both deeper interest and more serious efforts at analysis.

Encouraging thought about some of the long-range or fundamental issues of the political order is a fourth objective. The shape of actual or potential deep moral disagreements and their possible consequences, or the extent to which much policy confirms existing patterns of the distribution of wealth and power, are the kinds of matters that demand recurrent and thoughtful speculation from policymakers. Such thinking may help students to hear emerging ethical arguments more clearly or to identify new options for policy more responsive to the long-term needs of the political order.

Another goal for courses in ethics and policymaking is the familiarization of students with some of the traditions of ethical argument. A grounding in democratic theory, constitutional principles, and philosophic ethics generally will make available to students a variety of analytic tools and sources for reflection. An encounter with differing views will help students clarify their own ideas, and may encourage a measure of tolerance as well.

A final goal for the teaching of ethics has to do with the development of moral character; self-understanding and a lively sense of personal obligation are as supportive of good policymaking as they are valuable intrinsically. Here the limitations of what can be done in a classroom are plainest, but far from absolute. Opportunities can be offered, in discussion or writing, for the deepening of self-knowledge and for serious thinking about personal and policy commitments. Ways can be found to encourage participation, imaginatively or actually, in policy choices that test the values of those involved. Nor is character unaffected by the images that can be offered of acts and choices worthy of emulation; more than a few students are hungry for better aspirations.

C. Faculty

Some formal training in ethics, whether in philosophy, political theory, or social ethics, seems essential to adequate teaching about ethics and policymaking. So too does a considerable amount of knowledge about the substance of policy and about how it is made. Familiarity with other areas of policy analysis is extremely helpful, and a good background in history or in the law is also of great value. No discipline by itself offers training adequate to these needs, and many of those teaching in the field have commented on the weakness of their own preparation. There are, however, a considerable number of scholars who have been able to acquire the kinds of knowledge requisite to successful teaching.

The majority of those who teach ethics and policy courses have had extensive training in political theory. Their advantage is considerable. Political theorists have all had some graduate work in other aspects of political science, and they are likely to be knowledgeable about at least some aspects of the policy process. Even if their work has been largely in the history of political theory, they ordinarily know a good bit about the major modern ethical theories, and their understanding of utilitarianism and democratic theory is likely to be relatively deep.

Political theorists will usually be weaker in modern social philosophy than those who come to the field from philosophy departments, and neither group is as likely to be in touch with modern European ethical thought as are those whose field is social ethics. Some scholars in each of these areas have maintained a deep interest in contemporary American policy problems and issues, but those in social ethics, trained in departments of religion, seem to have done so with somewhat more consistency than the others.

Several programs have recently been developed that are aimed at extending the intellectual reach of faculty interested in teaching in the area of ethics and policymaking. Intensive and relatively brief summer seminars, these programs can indicate the shape of the necessary preparation; but the work that is needed represents a substantial additional commitment of time and energy. In our judgment, and as is recommended in the Report of the Hastings Center Project,[12] whatever one's background, the equivalent of at least a full year's graduate study in ethical theory and at least a full year's graduate study in public policy should be minimum requirements.

Fellowships subsidizing a year of study might be the best way to provide for the training of additional faculty members. Independent study of substantive issues and problems of official responsibility could be supplemented by courses where previous academic preparation is weak or nonexistent. Without such fellowships, the work of preparation can be accomplished by giving up time from other research, taking courses during the year in addition to fulfilling a normal teaching load, and spending summers in independent study.

Although we assume that political theorists will continue to do the largest share of teaching about ethics and politics, much may be gained by involving scholars from other fields. We hope that some who may be recruited for teaching will have philosophy backgrounds, others that of social ethics, still others history or the law. The importance of law and constitutional principles in determining the obligations of policymakers and in shaping policy makes the inclusion of some scholars with a legal education a particularly pressing need.[13]

Even with adequate preparation, those concerned with ethics and policy will often find themselves teaching outside of any area in which they can reasonably claim to be expert. Diversity of interest and the ability to study quickly, along with a willingness to rely on more expert colleagues, will be helpful. A talent for teaching jointly with colleagues from very different backgrounds can also be of considerable value.

III. Ethical Problems of Policymaking

Most policy has as its declared aim some public good; its conception and execution are shaped by rules, agreements, and ideals that have normative force in our political order. While the moral dimensions of policy warrant examination by analysts and decisionmakers as a general matter, strict scrutiny is justified under at least three circumstances: (1) when the duty of the official is unclear, either because of obligations that conflict, or because of a conflict between an obligation and legitimate self-interest; (2) when the extent to which particular values are embodied in alternative policy options is disputed or insufficiently understood; (3) when the norms or principles guiding policy are themselves unclear or contradictory.

These problems, of responsibility and of choice about conflicting values or in relation to the ultimate goals of policy, define the most important areas in which moral reasoning is appropriate and necessary to governmental actors. Accordingly, they are central to our discussion of ethical dilemmas in policymaking. Real decisions, of course, may simultaneously exemplify several different kinds of ethical dilemmas.[14]

Our purposes are both descriptive and evaluative. We shall try to depict in a reasonably comprehensive way the range of ethical dilemmas faced by policymakers and to prepare the ground for an analysis of various approaches to teaching students how to deal with such problems. The normative judgments we make are intended partly to illustrate ways of analyzing moral dilemmas in public decisionmaking. Let them also serve to suggest the sorts of ethical reasoning we think likely to be encouraged by the educational approaches we advance.

Because moral reasoning is fundamentally about the conscious choices of individuals in relation to actions affecting others, our emphasis in this paper is largely on individual choice. In the light of some of the major tendencies in modern policy analysis, this perhaps calls for some explanation. Many scholars argue persuasively that policy is not necessarily, or even usually, best explained as the logical outcome of a process in which costs and benefits of available options are carefully weighed by rational decisionmakers. Policies serve individual and group interests, they say, and constitute the means whereby organizations survive and prosper. Many of the loyalties, interests, and preconceptions that actually shape policy preferences, or that determine an organization's agenda, are at best only partly conscious in the minds of those who make decisions. Policy students are rightly warned that a "rational-actor model" of policymaking is likely to be hopelessly inadequate as the sole basis for explanations of official choice.[15]

According to this approach, our emphasis on the dilemmas of individual choice might seem archaic or marginal, concerned chiefly with those rare and less important decisions in which conscious individual choices are determinative. Such a judgment would be greatly mistaken. The fact is that a substantial portion of the important choices involved in large-scale policies are made by individuals acting consciously. Thoughtful histories of any period of American politics abound in examples of ethical dilemmas faced by individual decisionmakers. In short, the bureaucratic model explains only part of the story of governmental choice.[16]

The importance of individual choice in the policy process is, however, only part of the justification for our approach. A focus on individuals is all the more urgently needed because of the weight increasingly attributed to organizational factors in making and explaining decisions; individual moral reasoning can be a critical and countervailing resource in policy choice.

A. Dilemmas of Responsibility

In analyzing the ethical dilemmas of individual policymakers, the idea of responsibility must play a central role. Responsibility implies both discretion and accountability; policymakers have considerable freedom to act on behalf of others, but they must answer for their choices to superiors, colleagues, the courts, and the public at large.[17] As we intend it here, responsibility refers to the whole range of obligations assumed by promise or agreement, or imposed by law or procedure, and it includes as well a general obligation to exercise discretion wisely for the benefit of others. Such a view of responsibility is obviously akin to the idea of justice, the core meaning of which is the fulfillment of reasonable expectations.[18] Only those decisionmakers who act justly in the exercise of power, therefore, may be said to be responsible. Most of the obligations of policymakers are unproblematic: they can be discharged routinely and usually are.

Dilemmas arise for decisionmakers when responsibilities conflict, when the obligations they undertake or the rules to which they are subject are unclear, or when they are unsure how to weigh their responsibilities against personal needs or desires. While self-interest and moral uncertainty plague officials just as they do all other human beings, the obligations decisionmakers voluntarily assume pose especially perplexing moral challenges. Before examining some of the most significant of these difficulties, consider the main sources of those obligations.

As promises and agreements create reasonable expectations of performance or behavior, they establish obligations. To accept an office is ordinarily to promise fulfillment of its duties, whether or not the promise is verbal and solemn. In addition to the duties assumed by taking office, policymakers usually feel obligated by professional or scientific norms, or by promises made to secure appointment or election. A second category of obligations arises from the rules, procedural norms, and laws that shape political processes. Constitutional principles, statutes, standard operating procedures, precedents and custom, expectations of truthfulness and fair play may all be felt to be obligatory by those who have accepted public office. Political principles and ideals relating to the objectives of policy represent the third category of official obligations. Here the ordinary or *prima facie* duty of every human being to do good is burgeoned out for policymakers to include ideals such as peace, liberty, public tranquillity, or the general welfare. Personal moral codes, variously based on religion, philosophy, instinct, or tradition, may also impose standards or enjoin acts with as much force as any other rules.

Loyalties to political allies, governmental coworkers, friends, and family may all have a place among a policymaker's commitments. Similarly, loyalty may be felt to local or regional needs and desires, as well as to particular ethnic or communal groups. Such commitments or expectations may oblige, even if in their more limited application they are to be distinguished from broader responsibilities to the public as a whole.

Self-interest—one's own needs and desires, career hopes or personal ambitions—cannot properly be thought to oblige. Yet there is an appropriate space for the interests of the self, a space bounded but never obliterated by obligations assumed or imposed. The proper size of that space, the place of one's own interests whether or not in collision with one's duties, is most often a question that arises in the consideration of a choice to accept, or to impose, an obligation. Examining the extent to which self-interest is present in a decision may help to clarify and resolve conflicts among obligations.

The dilemmas that are inevitably created by these diverse obligations of policymakers are not usually simple conflicts between two competing duties. Most often, the hard choices are knotted of several of the strands of obligations noted above, woven together with questions about the proper balance between obligations and personal interests. Nor, it must be confessed, are all dilemmas of responsibility easily resolvable by moral reasoning, although attempts at resolution are a constant feature of the policymaking process. The analysis is made even more difficult, because in real dilemmas, the moral stakes are often not apparent. Sorting out and weighing the obligations are crucial to the task of adjudicating conflicts among them.

We must add, too, that duty is not the whole of morality. Beliefs about what is virtuous and honorable, or degrading and prohibited, are part of one's moral framework; how energetically we do good, with what friendliness and benevolence we regard our fellows, how kind and patient we are, and how we express our anger are all significant moral questions, no less for officials than for others. Qualities of character and aspiration[19] are not directly discussed in the examples that follow, but it should be noted that teaching about the ethical dilemmas of policymakers can effectively examine the ways these qualities affect decision-making, and can sometimes foster their development in students.

1. Conceptions of the public interest

Perhaps the most notorious conflicts of obligation are those that pit a policymaker's view of the public interest and the common good against what law or procedure require. Under which circumstances is it reasonable to argue that a view of the public interest, especially one that is shared by less than a majority, ought to have sufficient moral authority to justify a policymaker in overriding accepted legal or democratic procedures?

To answer this question even to a minimally adequate extent, we must digress for a moment to consider what is meant by "the public interest." Some have argued that the phrase is without any substantive content, or that it can signify nothing more than an aggregation of preferences expressed in a market system, or of votes in the policy process. Because we claim that serious conflicts can exist between procedural obligations of policymakers and their general duty to defend or advance the public interest, we feel it essential to address these objections.

The first question to be answered is whether the concept of the public interest makes sense. Twenty years ago, in political science at least, the view that it did not commanded wide support.[20] Some scholars, influenced by logical positivism, denied that normative concepts were amenable to logical argument. Others thought the notion vague, charging those who used the term with defining it in varying and mutually incompatible ways.

The struggle over the meaning of "the public interest" is in some ways a microcosm of the more general battle about the status of ethical argument that has been waged through the whole of this century. The charges of the positivists have been answered by a defense of ethical theory generally and by ably argued explications of normative notions of the public interest that defend its usefulness for studying and making policy.[21] Among the most effective of the postpositivist arguments are those that have drawn support from ordinary language philosophy.[22]

We agree with those who believe that normative debate and analysis are philosophically possible, and that debates about the public interest make sense. For us, politics is not only the arena of clashing interests; it is also the agora of opposing ideals. Policy choice emerges from private needs and desires, but it embodies judgments about the common good as well. The public interest, as the phrase is used in political debate, is the standard by which policy is judged. Assertions that a policy is in the public interest are properly defended with normative arguments. Reasons of fact and of principle are offered to convince others that the policy will have results that are desirable on a common or public, rather than a merely private, basis.

Agreement about the public interest is often present, although the great issues in this society are ones about which there is no such apparent consensus. Some disagreements are resolvable, others not; the minimum requirement of a particular public policy would seem to be that plausible reasons can be advanced for believing that it serves the public interest.

Policymakers and all other citizens may appropriately, on our view, form conceptions of the public interest. A question arises, however, as to whether such conceptions can be properly included among the obligations of officials. A substantial body of argument, especially from scholars in the field of public administration, holds that they cannot.[23] Various reasons are adduced for this view, but all share a commitment to the primacy of the political process. Scholars in the positivist tradition have argued for legislative determination about questions of value, holding that administrators have no special knowledge about ethical matters, and indeed that expert knowledge about ethics is in principle unavailable.[24] Others, committed to democratic values, have urged administrators to pursue substantive goals only when these are agreed upon, to follow agreed procedures if such exist and if there is no agreement on substantive ends, and to be guided by the results of political conflict when neither substantive nor procedural agreement is available.[25]

As guidelines for ordinary times (if there are such times), these might be plausible, but they seem hardly adequate to the multiple moral crises through which we have lived. For it is precisely in the circumstances of greatest disagreement, about civil liberties, civil rights, and Vietnam, that independent commitments and alternative views have been most important. At such times especially, we need officials who can be guided first by conscience, by devotion to views of the public good at odds with current outcomes of the political process and the present judgments of the citizenry. Theirs is the quality of moral leadership to which subsequent generations pay homage.

These admittedly intuitive judgments suggest that policymakers may have an obligation to the public interest that is separate from, and sometimes opposed to, the other obligations of office. What arguments can be advanced in support of this view, and can they keep within reasonable bounds any definition of the public interest that rises above the determinations of the political process?

Under at least three types of circumstances, policymakers are likely to be especially well placed to judge that the results of procedures and process are unlikely to produce optimal results and to take corrective action: (1) when the debate over policy is inadequate because important information is suppressed or ignored; (2) when policy makers have a superior understanding of the long-run consequences of particular policy alternatives; and (3) when the constitutive rules of the political process are being violated by others. In each type of situation, policymakers may be thought to have special responsibilities, and in each type it will be found that, on occasion, the obligations of a policymaker to the public interest may collide with the more specific procedural duties of his or her office.

2. Procedural obligations and the public good

Deceptions, leaks, insubordination, and official lawbreaking are often defended on the basis of the claim that they are in the public interest. When and how are such claims likely to be convincing?

In the previous section we suggested that policymakers may have reason to believe that their independent judgments of the public interest may be truer to the public good than the determinations of a political process deformed by poor debate or by the exclusion of important interests. A more difficult question now presents itself. Can such an independently held and admittedly uncertain view of the public interest impose obligations strong enough to conflict seriously with the explicit and recognized obligations of officials to law and procedure or with the ordinary obligations of individuals to truthfulness?

At the most general level, it might be thought that policy-makers ought to go beyond the obligations of advocacy or special care, even to the extent of violating procedural norms and laws, on behalf of groups excluded by weakness or discrimination from participation in debate. But it is in the nature of the case that such efforts cannot be maintained for very long, except in cases where sufficient popular support is already available to change procedures or laws. The poor and the weak, moreover, are especially dependent on procedural rights for their protection. Acts undertaken in their behalf that simultaneously undermine adherence to law and procedure may therefore result in a net loss.

Before turning to more specific problems, it may be helpful to survey those circumstances under which conflicts of the sort we are considering are most likely to arise. The first of these is a crisis or emergency.

In emergencies, important values such as national survival or security may appear to be suddenly threatened by dangers not envisaged by laws or regulations that prevent a prompt and adequate response. This justification for lawbreaking may often be convincing, but it poses some obvious dangers. The claim of emergency may be used to prevent any thoughtful consideration of the issues at stake. While the claim can be valid, it is often false, designed to stampede officials and citizens and to silence the legitimate objections of opponents.

Obligations to the public interest may also have precedence over procedural requirements when particular officials possess superior knowledge, unavailable to (or unrecognized by) the electorate, the legislature, or their superiors. This justification is most persuasive when it can be shown that the official's knowledge would change the minds of those to whom one owes a duty, were they privy to the same information. For this reason, it is only likely to be convincing in circumstances where time for persuasion is lacking.

A third important variety of justification on public-interest grounds for the breaking of rules of laws is the claim that they are vague or contradictory in their commands. If this is so, then it is not possible to know with certainty what conduct is required, and a view of the public interest may appear a more convincing guide to action. Because of the frequency with which official deception, leaks, insubordination, and official lawbreaking have been defended in recent years as in the public interest, each warrants a closer examination.

a. Deception

The imagery of our politics is borrowed from war and football; as Vince Lombardi said, "Winning isn't everything—it's the only thing." Strategy depends on power, maneuver, ambition, loyalty, surprise, and deception. There are rules, of course, for war and football and politics, and in football there are referees. We know winning isn't really everything.[26]

The temptations of deception in politics and policymaking are enormous. In the short run, opponents can be bamboozled and voters confused, elections won and laws passed. For a while, at least, the costs of programs can be underestimated and benefits exaggerated in order to secure the support of administrators or congressional commmittees. Even the most reckless charges against the opposition will have an audience. And there are ready excuses. Effectiveness and the public good, loyalty, and the preservation of privacy may all be advanced in defense of a lie. The people, it may be added, want to be lied to (or at least they would approve, if they knew).

In the long run, there is usually less advantage and more harm. One by one, deceptions undermine the capacity for debate and erode the credibility of the government. Individuals who lose their reputation for veracity usually cannot accomplish very much. Paradoxically, the people, who sometimes do indeed want to be lied to, nevertheless resent it when the lies are discovered. Their ability to evaluate or influence policy, even to consent meaningfully, is lost.

The damage done by official deception, by the "credibility gap" or the lies of Watergate, is evident; but the barriers to it still seem weak. Why should this be so? One reason is ingrained expectations; no one counts on candor from a press secretary. Another deeper cause is suggested by the images of combat with which we began. Like most people, Americans enjoy combat, and we are often delighted by deception. Making fools of the enemy may be as much fun as doing them in. The joys of deception, of fooling others, are among the pleasures of power. Ordinarily, all this is harmless, fooling children, dogs, friends, and lovers with innocent untruths. We enjoy childlike pleasure in being fooled, tricked, outsmarted—yet would not be betrayed. Thus we are ambivalent about the deceptions of our leaders. There is something attractive about Lyndon Johnson passing good bills in the Senate by guile and deception, something attractive even about the survival by electoral machination of "Landslide Lyndon" in the changing landscape of Texas politics. The vicarious joy is greater in Franklin D. Roosevelt's wily and successful stratagems against enemies foreign and domestic. But the price of these pleasures can be high. The fateful deceptions of the 1964 campaign owed something to Johnson's mentor, FDR, and to the false campaign promise in 1940 not to send American boys into any foreign wars.[27]

The obvious short-term advantages of particular lies and the great costs of the patterns of deception will continue to create ethical dilemmas for policymakers. Some of the more common of these are indicated here, along with a few comments about the ways they may be resolved.

False promises by candidates are a recurrent feature of our political scene. FDR's 1932 pledge to balance the budget has a strikingly familiar ring. Candidates who declare their fealty to the 25 cent fare, or to a reduction in the size of the bureaucracy, or to no increase in taxes are often returned to office in spite of their reversals. Nor is it easy to know how the circle might be broken. Voters make contradictory demands and crude judgments, and they respond to symbolic issues. Candor is hard to detect and not always rewarded when discovered.

The deceptions of public relations are similarly well entrenched. There may be some "virtue" in having a press secretary to deny awkward facts so that his principal may speak less often and more truthfully. A less disputable advantage in having someone in charge of press relations is that questions can be more effectively anticipated and alternatives to deception more carefully examined. Attacks from opponents, moreover, require some defense. The real trick is to keep advocacy and apology from falling over the brink of downright lying.

In a crisis, the need for deception may be compelling. Enemies in real wars must often be misled, and even in peacetime there may be nothing but a lie between justice and an angry mob. When the Chancellor of the Exchequer was asked in Parliament whether Great Britain would leave the gold standard, his answer, only a few days before the nation was to do so, was a straightforward denial that he knew to be false. He saw no alternative that would avoid confusion and illicit profits, although advance planning might have given him one.[28]

The value of a lie in a crisis depends on its being believed, so if this justificiation must be invoked often, it will defeat itself. For this reason, the long-lasting crises of our time, for example, aspects of the Cold War, justify or excuse few lies. Durable falsifications about important matters are rare. Only a few can be maintained over time, and often then only at the cost of steadily extending and deepening the deception.[29]

In the pursuit of pressing political goals, crisis may be invoked to justify the twisting or invention of facts; in a similar manner, it has been argued that the elusiveness or unavailability of facts is itself a justification for lying. On reflection this hardly seems convincing. MacNamara's faked statistics in support of his position on Vietnam made fair debate more difficult within the administration.[30] His hypothetical, orderly "truths" met the test of competition, while genuine ignorance and partial, contradictory knowledge looked "soft." Those who were convinced were fooled and rendered less able to cope with changing realities.

Lies to prevent embarrassment to oneself or one's friends are common. Privacy can ordinarily be protected as well by silence, but on occasion, only a lie may be available to foreclose embarrassing questions or harsh criticism. Such lies are usually told to cover up misdeeds. If the crimes are those of others, the lie makes us accessories, and if our own, the lie compounds them. Where the need is great and the loyalty strong, such lies may be excusable, though hardly justifiable. When what is concealed is not wrongdoing, on the other hand, but weakness or vulnerability, falsehoods may be more defensible. Concealing bastardy, for example, might not be harmful to anyone; lying to protect such a secret is injurious only to the practice of truthtelling—which is not to say that it is costless. Lying about an official's alcoholism, on the other hand, is much more problematic.

Lies told to conceal religious heterodoxy or to screen adultery or homosexuality may also be defended. What right, it is asked, does the public have to know such things? Concealment, however, is normally possible without lying, and, when it is impossible, lying often does not help. Deception may always be discovered; if it is about something interesting or someone important, discovery is more likely, a likelihood that appears to be increasing.

The temptation to lie about an opponent is always great, especially when one has been attacked with lies. "He did it first" has never been an acceptable justification for giving in to the temptation, however. A liar may have little claim to truth, but the lie is not told to the liar alone.[31]

Indirect deceptions may be as tempting as lies. Withholding needed information from opponents or allowing misinterpretations of one's words to stand without correction may be effective tactics. By silence and studied ambiguity, General Charles De Gaulle encouraged his ministers and generals to deceive themselves during the final phase of the Algerian war. In doing so, he may well have saved France from civil war.[32] The praise he won for these acts is largely deserved, but the costs were awesome and in some part avoidable. Moslems remaining loyal to France were betrayed by De Gaulle's policy when they were slaughtered by the new regime with little French effort to save their lives. General Challe, who promised in good faith to protect these people, found his pledges utterly dishonored; in reaction to what he rightly regarded as De Gaulle's betrayal, Challe tragically agreed to lead a hopeless putsch.[33] Not all of De Gaulle's deceptions in this period can be justified. Surely his voicing of the *Algérie française* slogan, during one emotional moment in Oran, communicated an unnecessary pledge to the *pied noirs* that he knew would have to be betrayed. But some of De Gaulle's deceptive strategy was probably needed to maintain the security of France.

The circumstances are rarely as extreme, and deception is rarely as justifiable. But it is often successful, and the temptation remains. Just this once, in this "crisis" and for that important object, the arguments run, and they are supported by a legitimate doubt that policymakers ought ever to prize moral purity above doing good. The most persuasive pressures to deceive, and the ones demanding the most careful analysis, are the arguments of the public good.

The possibility of a genuine dilemma must be admitted. Some lies may on balance be justifiable, even if no consequential lie is ever totally free of costs. What is needed is a fair-minded evaluation of the whole range of likely effects on policy, on liars and their opponents, on the public, and on the practice of truth-telling itself. Possible and long-term consequences should be fairly estimated, with the gravity of potential evils discounted—but not ignored—in proportion to their improbability.

Special caution is needed about conflict and war. It is easy to call a man an enemy, but not all foes are Hitler, Mussolini, or Tojo. While propaganda may help the war effort, its deceptions can sap the foundations of any peace that follows, as Woodrow Wilson found to his dismay.[34]

With foresight, lies can usually be avoided. When candor seems too costly, evasion is preferable to deceit.[35] Both may be discovered, but the public rightly finds deception less forgivable.

Lies will continue to be told, and be approved by many as well. The current debate in legal ethics about the status of deception reveals how deeply reasonable persons can differ on the issue.[36] In our increasingly adversarial society, the deceptions of investigative reports are often praised and may sometimes be needed, even though they surely impose costs in the form of bureaucratic defensiveness and may undermine the prestige of truth itself.

The worst lies are probably the unexpected ones. When in 1967 President Johnson deceived congressional leaders and his economic advisers about the war's cost and the possibilities of a tax increase, a whole new level of presidential deception was attained.[37] The strategy worked for a short while in securing both guns and butter, but with disastrous results for the party, the economy, the soldiers, the Vietnamese, and the credibility of the government.

b. Leaks

The leaking of legitimately secret information is a common and significant violation of procedural rules. It is perhaps the most

usual case of a conflict between objective legal or ethical obligations and one's personal conception of the public good. Under
what circumstances may one's sense of what the public good
requires be sufficient to justify the procedural violation?

When information essential to informed public debate about
important issues has been kept hidden unnecessarily, and when
no other means is available to give that information to the public,
leaks may be justified. Overclassification of information is endemic in government, and declassification by leaks to the press is
common.

Not all leaks are consequential, of course. The effectiveness of
the leak depends on the interest of some influential segment of
the people. Someone has to care, has to be shocked by what is
revealed; and the news must be spread.[38] Some leaks, on the
other hand, may have very dangerous consequences, risking the
integrity of governmental processes where confidentiality is essential. The apparent weakening of the government's capacity to
gather intelligence, stemming from the wholesale leaks as well as
unwarranted exposés of recent years, must surely be a cause for
concern.

Leaks are a constant feature of official life in Washington.
Real secrecy about important and controversial decisions is hard
to maintain even for a short time, a circumstance that may have
great costs, particularly in the area of foreign policy. Secrecy
during the early phase of the Nixon-Kissinger negotiations with
China was such that no advance word of changing U.S. policy
toward China was given to the Japanese government. The result
was an unfortunate shock to our most valuable allies in the
Pacific.

Individual acts of leaking are generally without great consequences for the spread of the practice of leaking in general, but
some leaks can be expected to produce broad effects, and these
require considerably more in the way of justification. Disclosures
about an organization that has hitherto been able to maintain
secrecy, for example, the CIA, can have immense consequences,
many of them clearly contrary to the public interest.

c. Insubordination

In most governmental organizations, an official's responsibility
for carrying out the legitimate orders and instructions of superior

officials is clear. Yet the refusal to obey is not uncommon, and is sometimes defended as being required by the public good. Under what circumstances can the obligation to one's view of the public interest be reasonably thought to justify insubordination? Two famous cases of official disobedience involving General Douglas MacArthur are suggestive.

After the invasion of Luzon in 1944, contrary to the wishes of his superiors and acting at times against their orders, General MacArthur successfully liberated several of the Philippine Islands. He did so because he believed he knew best what was required, and there is reason to believe that he was right. He understood better than Washington the deep sense of betrayal broken American promises had produced in the Philippines and believed bypassing the remaining islands would only increase that sense.[39] MacArthur's motives were undoubtedly mixed. There were deep personal reasons for his actions, among them great pride and a desire to atone for his failures in 1941. Yet the insubordination was successful in achieving some good ends, although among its costs one would have to weigh its precedental effect on MacArthur's later and less defensible disobedience.

Six years later in Korea, MacArthur was also sure that he was better informed than his commander-in-chief, and by a pattern of insubordinate behavior, he challenged the Truman-Acheson policy of limited war. In this case, however, no reasonable claim could have been advanced that the military and civilian authorities in Washington lacked as good a basis for judgment as he had. His information was no better than theirs, especially about global matters. His only (inadequate) justification could be that he understood better how to interpret it.[40]

Military insubordination in periods of crisis is not uncommon, and it may win subsequent praise. Field commanders, even platoon leaders, may see, or see more clearly, opportunities and dangers invisible or obscure to their superiors. The certainty of later review and the likelihood that unwise insubordinate acts will count heavily against career advancement tend to place reasonable limits on such acts.

MacArthur's reconquest of the Philippines may be defended from this point of view and also from another. What he did was in fact reviewable as it was happening. His disobedience could have been reversed by depriving him of his command or even simply by insisting on the orders given. The decision not to do so may be seen as tacit approval for his actions. Even MacArthur's performance in Korea has some claim to justification. Insubordination that openly courts dismissal is a way of emphasizing one's disagreement with policy in the strongest possible way. Commerce Secretary Henry Wallace's open dissent in 1945 about the Soviet Union, against President Harry S. Truman's wishes, is a similar case.[41] Such acts transform the procedural violation of insubordination into an ultimatum—"change the policy, or fire me and take the consequences."

Hidden insubordination owing to principled disagreement seems, by contrast, almost impossible to defend. The refusal on principle to fulfill an order carries with it the obligation to present that principle for scrutiny by one's superiors and sometimes by the public. Such cases must be distinguished, however, from the failure to execute orders issued casually or where, for symbolic purposes, failures of execution are expected and tacitly approved.

Finally it might be added that some orders and instructions are known to be unauthorized, in which case disobedience is almost always permissible. And when what is commanded is both wrong and illegal, disobedience may be obligatory.

d. Official lawbreaking

Lincoln's suspension of habeas corpus in the West during the Civil War seems in hindsight to have been unnecessary. National security was not sufficiently at risk from his Copperhead opponents to justify the clear and wholesale suspension of a constitutional right. Similarly the internment of Japanese-Americans during World War II deprived citizens of fundamental rights, not because of acts or known intentions, but because of supposed risks to national security represented by their racial ties. Surely, in hindsight, this was wrong. Weighing the risks prospectively is much harder. National security is not the only value, but it may be preeminent when threatened, and then we want our leaders to protect it vigorously.[42]

President Truman's seizure of the steel mills was defended also by the principle of national security, but the Supreme Court invalidated the justification because he had recourse to other clearly legal options that would have preserved essential production. The Constitution is not a suicide pact, but that incontrovertibly logical principle justifies only genuinely necessary departures from its dictates.[43] What is necessary, however, must often be weighed in little time by officials under great pressure.

The amount of lawbreaking actually required by national security is likely to be very small. Most threats can be anticipated, and defenses against them made legal. Yet it seems certain that officials will sometimes find themselves faced with circumstances where law is at variance with the requirements of security. What guidelines can be given these officials? How can abuses of the national security justification be prevented? Cases like Truman's can safely be left to the courts. The possibility of national security hysteria, however, remains with us, though no present issue seems likely to provoke it. When law is ineffective against an angry or frightened mob, the only additional safeguard is official courage, people who are willing to defend the law and stake their political hopes, if any, on the chance of an eventual return to sanity.

The most difficult choices will probably continue to be in the areas of intelligence and counterespionage. Undoubtedly, clear standards of permitted and prohibited actions, as well as more thorough and more systematic oversight, can limit some abuses. Yet such procedural restraints are notoriously hard to fashion; the history of congressional intelligence oversight suggests that, like the regulatory commissions, oversight committees will quickly lose their critical zeal. Procedures effective in preventing abuses, moreover, may impede the essential functions of intelligence.

Rules that force both broader consultation inside intelligence agencies, along with some outside review, especially by courts and legislators, may well be worth the risk. It is true that the more broadly information is shared, the more likely it is to leak. But such leaks are possible in any case, and likely only when there is serious controversy. The leaker presumes public outrage at what is being done or proposed and sees a danger that outweighs pledges of secrecy and the risk of damage to the intelligence apparatus. It is hard to imagine proposals for lawbreaking that are genuinely compelled by national security which would occasion such opposition.

The disclosures of recent years have clearly weakened morale in the intelligence community, and effectiveness has no doubt been somewhat diminished. Part of this happened, however, because the CIA had continued to function in the 1960s as if the unanimity of understanding and ideology in relation to America's enemies, which had characterized earlier periods, still prevailed. A showdown was to be expected, and far worse ones than we eventually had can be imagined. The most valuable safeguards against future abuses may be the altered consciousness of the intelligence agencies about the views of citizens and their representatives, coupled with a continuing open debate about the assumptions under which the intelligence community operates.

Should official discretion ever reach so far as to permit the breaking of laws on any public interest grounds other than national security? In crisis, again, the answer may be affirmative. While an obligation to reasonable caution is present for automobile drivers at all times, no one expects slavish obedience to red lights on the way to the emergency room. What of other times?

In the midst of the celebrated Ballinger-Pinchot controversy, and just prior to his dismissal for insubordination by President William H. Taft, Chief Forester Gifford Pinchot wrote that: "A public officer is bound first to obey the law and keep within it. But he is also bound, at any personal risk, to do everything the law will let him do for the public good."[44] This was somewhat disingenuous. Pinchot bent laws and procedures quite far at times. Fewer than five months before writing these words he had told the National Irrigation Congress that strict construction of the laws "necessarily favors the great interests as against the people ....The great oppressive trusts exist because of subservient lawmakers and adroit legal constructions."[45] The letter quoted earlier was itself a defense of an instance of whistle-blowing. In it Pinchot argued on behalf of two subordinates clearly guilty of violating administrative regulations in abetting the exposure of questionable though not clearly illegal practices in the Interior Department.[46]

At the close of Theodore Roosevelt's term in office, and with his approval, Pinchot masterminded the "withdrawal from entry" of some additional millions of acres of public lands he and Roosevelt feared would be gained illegitimately by power companies and exploited without public control. The dubious factual pretexts for those withdrawals were that the lands represented ranger station sites or that they were needed for reclamation projects. Neither justification could reasonably account for any substantial portion of the withdrawals,[47] and the only legal argument available to support the withdrawals was the doctrine that the president has a "supervisory power" to protect public lands from wrongful acquisition. Taft and Secretary of the Interior Ballinger thought the withdrawals illegal and reversed them. Although by Pinchot's effective protests they were largely restored, Taft and Ballinger have had many defenders on the issue.

The actions of Roosevelt and Pinchot in stretching the laws by very loose construction nevertheless may be justified by considerations of long-range public interest and the expectation of future agreement. They estimated that the strength of their political opponents did not accurately reflect the latent commitments of the public to conservationist views, and the public protest that restored the results of their work might seem to have proved them right. It is important to note that they struggled to avoid breaking the law and stayed (or almost stayed?) within its letter. Then, too, they acted in the expectation of review. Both the succeeding administration and the Congress had the power to overturn their acts.

Presidential decisions of this kind are not fully analogous to those faced by other government officials, in part because the President is an elected executive whose function it is to initiate legislation, as well as to implement it. Activist presidents have gone beyond their specific statutory authority since the time of the Louisiana Purchase. Laws are often stretched or evaded, and sometimes violated, in pursuit of their views of the public interest.

Yet presidential actions are largely reviewable by the Congress, and where actions contrary to law are not opposed by additional legislation (or, more rarely, by impeachment proceedings), congressional consent can often be inferred.[48] Congressional control over executive action may be supplemented by judicial action: the courts eventually held President Richard Nixon's massive impoundments of appropriated funds illegal despite the existence of precedents from earlier administrations.

Whether the public interest can override clear law is perhaps too abstract a question. Real dilemmas are more accurately captured by asking whether one's conception of the public interest can override clear law. In suggesting that it can in emergencies, appeal is made to notions of the public interest on which there is agreement. When there is disagreement, the question is a harder one.

3. Democracy and obligation

Administrators and legislators only occasionally face dramatic conflicts between procedural responsibilities and the public interest. Every day, however, they must cope with choices that require them to harmonize or even to choose between various kinds of obligations. All high officials, both elected and appointed, have some discretion, and many have a great deal. What are the appropriate standards for the exercise of this discretion?

The most common answer has been that choices among conflicting values ought to be made according to a theory of democracy. While there is disagreement about what version of democratic philosophy is most persuasive, a broad consensus exists that both legislative and executive judgment ought to reflect the will of the people. The appropriate ways to accomplish this end have been a principal subject of debate in the literature of public administration and in the vast body of writing about the subject of representation.

Here we can only comment on a few of the ethical dilemmas that arise as officials, in the exercise of discretion, make choices that are shaped by democratic norms and by other obligations. With some regret, we find we must leave aside completely the interesting and important structural questions about discretion: whether, for example, party responsibility or caucus control should be encouraged in the Congress; to what extent legislative responsibility can be altered by campaign finance legislation; how governmental reorganization or changes in the merit system might affect administrative ethics; or whether efforts should be made to reduce sharply the areas of administrative discretion. For reasons of space our discussion is limited to the dilemmas of actors in the existing system, but we intend no unqualified endorsement of the status quo.

a. Representation

Contradictory obligations are built into our notions of representation. While a precise adjudication of the conflicts elected representatives face is only rarely possible, reflection and analysis may encourage more responsiveness to the whole range of obligations to which they are subject.

The problem is an important one. The dilemmas of representation are not only matters of legislative responsbility; similar problems are present as well in the life of every official whose tasks are partly representative in nature. The classic legislator's quandary opposes his or her free exercise of judgment about the public interest to the mandate of his or her constituency. We may join Burke in endorsing independence or Mill in a more democratic and responsive view of legislative duty. In either case, however, we are forced to recognize that both kinds of obligation are ordinarily present.[49]

The primary legislative imperative, then, would seem to be discovering ways of fulfilling both sorts of duties. Alternatives must be sought that meet both the needs and wants of constituents and the legislator's view of sound policy; options must be developed that serve both local and national needs. And sometimes legislators ought to teach, bringing neglected facts and ignored arguments to the attention of voters in such a way that they can be induced to support, or at least tolerate, votes contrary to their original desires.

Such a view of legislative responsibility may be decried by those who believe the political system most faithfully expresses the public's judgments and achieves the public good when legislators are most responsive to their constituents and most concerned with their political self-interest. On this view, based on a depiction of politics as the mere struggle of competing interests, legislators have no special duty of moral reflection, no need to ponder the common good.

Such a position seems to us unconvincing. If politics is as much debate about common good as it is competition about private needs and wants, then the role of legislators in promoting and carrying on that debate seems essential. The attack on the notion of legislative responsibility, with its emphasis on the political calculations of representatives, does, however, suggest a useful caution. Representatives are, in fact, limited in the extent to which they can support conceptions of the public interest that diverge sharply from those of their supporters. On rare occasions, and especially in emergencies, we may conclude that a representative's duty to the common good justifies taking a great risk of future defeat; we may even argue that assuming such a risk can be obligatory in meeting the educative duties of legislative office. Nevertheless, in the long run, representatives can hardly be expected to defend views of the public interest seriously at odds with those of the voters. Instead, those citizens with alternative views of the common good must organize support for candidates with whom they agree.

Beyond the "mandate-independence" controversy there are other questions to be raised about the obligations of a representative. Are promises to the electorate to be understood as binding? Is a change of party identification an instance of promise-breaking to voters or to supporters? When is such a change defensible? How much of a legislator's energy ought to be devoted to analyzing the issues he or she faces, and how much to constituency services that might help in winning elections? How much effort should be devoted to the symbolic dimensions of a representative's role, and when is it appropriate to trade instrumental goals for symbolic ones on behalf of one's constituency?

b. Administrative discretion

When the President initiates a bill subsidizing agricultural production and then later signs some version of that bill into law, it is clear that policy is being made. So, too, are the authoritative decisions of government at other levels rightly called policy, even down to the choice of the policemen on the beat to enforce or not to enforce a particular law.

Most administrative acts are partly shaped according to rules made by legislatures, but administrators do make policy. That is to say, they do more than simply execute legislative decisions; they exercise discretion in the decisions they make. Administrative discretion is a necessity of modern government,[50] and it seems to us not incompatible with democracy. It may, however, have the effect of obscuring some important ethical dimensions of policy. In making significant choices about people's lives—about who survives or moves or pays—officials may be guided by only the most general purposes for which discretion was granted; how, in such circumstances, are ethical decisions to be made?

Several scholars who have considered the subject have argued that the ethical obligations of public officials are most effectively met by adherence to the principle of democracy.[51] By this has been meant in the first place a steady respect for the determinations of legitimate political processes—a consciousness not only of laws, but of the purposes for which legislatures have granted discretion. Second, the democratic principle has been seen as requiring a respect for hierachical organization. Decisions should, it is argued, be considered at the highest possible level, where "perceptions are necessarily broader, less technical and expert, more political."[52]

More recently it has been argued that, in addition, those who exercise discretion have an equal obligation to a principle of procedural fairness. On this view, minimum procedural requirements include: (1) that affected parties and the public be notified before decisions are made; (2) that affected parties have access to fair and unbiased forums for debate; and (3) that provision be made for appeal from decisions to an independent body for review.[53]

These views, which we regard as persuasive, suggest an important range of ethical dilemmas. Obligation to respect the political process may well conflict with these procedural duties of fairness to those who are the objects of policymaking. And the duty of energetic adherence to the purposes for which discretion exists may conflict with both. The politics of highway building or dam and waterway construction are replete with conflicts such as these. Fair hearings are often delayed until after important decisions are made, out of fear that controversy and review will make projects impossible to complete. Political processes mandate a particular course of action, but full processes of notice, hearings, and review frustrate the decision.

It seems to us clear that in facing these dilemmas many policymakers have chosen to emphasize political responsibility and policy effectiveness at the expense of fair procedures. While such choices are often defensible, the costs need to be weighed with great care. Since administrative discretion seems questionable in the light of popularly accepted democratic notions of legislative control, official acts imposed on individuals and communities without adequate notice or hearings, and without possibility of independent review, may appear intolerably arbitrary and can be destructive of faith in the political process.

Failure to adhere scrupulously to the requirements of fair procedures may have other negative consequences, because administrators cannot by themselves adequately estimate the social and human costs of the alternative policy options before them. The particular responses of affected parties to arguments of cost and benefit, or right and wrong, can be of great use in improving the quality of decisions. New alternatives can be discovered, and ways developed to satisfy needs and objections originally neglected.

A common reaction to procedures designed to guarantee fairness is that they are at best a necessary evil, and at worst, "red tape,"[54] far more likely to frustrate policymaking than to improve it. While this may sometimes be true, it strikes us that one reason fairness requirements delay decisions is that they are so often met insincerely, and at too late a stage in the decision process. When fair hearing and review requirements are invoked by parties unfairly frozen out of the crucial decision processes, the stage is set for protracted and bitter conflict. Policymakers who are sure that their analysis has identified the right choice are bound to be impatient with any opposition. Those who are less sure, who genuinely seek the wisdom of persons who will care about or be affected by the outcomes, may learn much through the procedures designed to guarantee fairness, and may in addition forge more cohesive support for the policies they choose.

The obligation to fair procedures is nevertheless only one of a policymaker's responsibilities. Nor is responsibility adequately defined when obligations to have respect for both the results of political processes and the norms of hierarchical control are included. Those who exercise discretion must also weigh the duty of beneficence, and perhaps that of compassion,[55] when they are making choices that affect the lives of others.

4. Public duty, personal morality, and private interest

Until now, we have looked chiefly at conflicts *among* official obligations. We turn here to those dilemmas created when public responsibilities are opposed by other obligations, or by self-interest. It seems to us clear that ordinary moral duties, such as promise-keeping or loyalty to friends and family, can sometimes rightly be honored even when they conflict with procedural obligations of officials or with their general duty to the public interest. So too, on rare occasions, can considerations of self-interest justify the failure to fulfill official responsibilities. What are some of the ways such conflicts may be decided?

A fair-minded approach requires first of all that the competing obligations and interests be stated clearly. Self-interested solidarity should not, for example, be miscalled an obligation of loyalty. Clarity is necessary if reasoned argument is to have any hope of adequately weighing the competing moral claims. A second question to be raised in such conflicts is that of an alternative. Obligations incompatible with official duty should not ordinarily be accepted. If they have been, resignation from office may be an honorable way of coping with the conflict. In some circumstances, however, especially when time is short, resignation may simply be a blameworthy failure to fulfill the duties of office.

In what follows we have cataloged some of the more important of the diverse circumstances under which conflicts of this general type occur. Some important problems have been omitted. Among these are the ethical problems of officials in advisory roles,[56] some of the dimensions of organizational loyalty, problems of the unionization of government employees,[57] and problems of the legitimate use of professional expertise and professional reputation in advising on policy.

a. Public good and moral duties

The requirements of a personally held idea of moral duty may clash directly with judgments of the public interest based on utilitarian and democratic standards. Officeholders who hold other moral views may feel on occasion that the obligations they have undertaken require acts against their own consciences. The options may be stark: to violate conscience, to act against the public interest, or to resign from office. Whether or not it is philosophically coherent to hold such a position has been much debated,[58] but it seems evident that many do hold it. Political action, it is believed, often and necessarily involves officeholders in immoral acts. They must deceive and fight and sometimes kill for their objectives—acts which are, on this view, reprehensible no matter how valuable the ends.

Such a way of seeing the moral circumstances of policymaking is attractive, because the guilt engendered may tend to limit immoral acts, and to encourage efforts toward atonement and reconciliation. It serves to emphasize the tragic dimensions of political choice, and insists that costs be felt and remembered, even when they are outweighed by benefits. Yet this view may also carry with it a worrisome contrary tendency. The belief that politics is inevitably involved in wrongdoing may have the effect of weakening the demand that each deviation from procedural norms and rules ought to be weighed and tested. Political acts do indeed often have unavoidably tragic consequences, and it may be not be unreasonable to speak sometimes of doing wrong in order to do good, but this should not lead to any lowering of our standards and expectations about official responsibility.[59]

Promises made for the performance of actions contrary to official responsibility pose some of the hardest problems in this area. It may often be reasonable to argue that such promises should not have been made, or because the negative consequences were not foreseen, that they should not oblige. But when promises have been made, they are supported by the fact that the obligation to keep promises is among the most important generally accepted obligations. Personal honor may demand that the fulfillment of a promise take precedence over public responsibility.[60] When this is the case, guilt may be appropriate whatever the choice, and remorse may teach effectively the lessons of careful promising.

b. Disagreement

Ethical problems stemming from disagreement within organizations are both common and important. How strongly should one object to policies with which one disagrees? When should disagreement be limited? To what lengths should one go in expressing one's disagreement within an organization? When and how is one justified in making disagreement public, or at least evident, to some persons outside of one's organization?

In the face of a serious difference of opinion, one can be silent or disagree openly or resign; but it seems obvious that the exit-voice-loyalty paradigm is too brief a description of the complex options open to those who dissent.[61] Opposition can mean speaking up among one's colleagues or speaking out to the interested public. It can mean resisting or being insubordinate or engaging in sabotage. Sorting out one's responsibilities requires understanding the available possibilities and their implications.

Protest is usually strong disagreement. In some organizations, merely to circulate a dissenting memorandum among one's colleagues would be protest; in others, nothing short of outright public criticism or resignation might qualify. A protest may be effective partly because it is unusual—it changes the ordinary pattern of discussion and decisionmaking, and may force reconsideration or the examination of neglected alternatives. Violating the norms of expected behavior may also have the opposite effect. Anger at the protest may harden commitments to the existing policy. Whether a protest has a chance of being effective depends in part on how those in charge react to it.

When verbal protest inside an organization is inadequate, other strategies are available. Disagreement can become opposition, orchestrating internal protests and providing additional evidence or argument for opposing points of view. One may find support outside one's own agency or office.[62] Resistance, from slowdown tactics and nonenforcement to outright insubordination, is also possible, and sometimes can defeat a policy or mitigate its perceived negative effects.

Resignation, or the threat of resignation, can be a way of testifying to the seriousness or the strength of one's conviction that a policy is wrong. Other sorts of overt refusals or noncompliance may have a similar effect when they openly expose the official to the risk of being fired or demoted or reassigned. Threatening resignation does not ordinarily involve deception or violations of rules or procedure, as resistance and slowdown tactics often do. Yet actually resigning means removing oneself from the theater of action and giving up the ability to influence a policy from within. It may also impose severe financial hardship or foreclose career opportunities.

All of these possible forms of diagreement can take place inside organizations, but frequently protest that begins internally becomes public controversy. When large stakes, powerful interests, or important procedural or substantive values are involved, both opponents and supporters of a policy may try to mobilize support on the outside. In such circumstances, tactics that may pose dilemmas for policymakers include leaking or openly giving out hitherto secret information, as well as resignation accompanied by protest.

The decision to make disagreement public may be attacked as disloyal and subversive of the long-range needs and purposes of an organization. In political orders that value democratic control and open public debate, such charges are usually unpersuasive, although it seems clear enough that public criticism will often reduce a critic's effectiveness within an organization. The open airing of internal differences, moreover, can, on occasion, genuinely weaken organizational morale and reduce the capacity to accomplish objectives.

c. Corruption

Corruption is official wrongdoing for private advantage for oneself or one's family or friends. In itself it poses no ethical dilemma, at least for most American decisionmakers. In countries where family and tribal ties are strong by comparison with the central government, and the future is uncertain, patterns that seem to us corrupt might be more defensible.[63] The dilemmas arising out of corruption are principally those of how a policymaker reacts to it. Graft and bribery aren't vanishing species. Though some old-fashioned forms of boodling may have disappeared, there is no reason to believe that corruption is on the way to extinction.[64] When one encounters corruption, especially among one's friends, there may be moral incentives to tolerate it or sometimes even actively to conceal it.

Fighting corruption takes resources that might be put to use elsewhere, and it is nearly always an unattractive fight. Some good headlines for the fighter may be produced, but so will more news about official malfeasance. Morale in investigated agencies may sag, and public cynicism about government may increase. Nor will the fight ever be victorious. A good battle can reduce corruption, not eliminate it, and the advantage gained may not last long.

It seems likely, on the other hand, that the recurrent crusades against corruption are important in keeping it within limits. The negative effects of corruption investigations may only multiply with delay. Not to fight corruption is to risk being known as soft on graft, an unenviable tag at best, and an encouragement to the grafters.[65] When one lacks the authority to investigate, the temptation to tolerate endemic corruption may be much greater. In many cities illegal payments appear needed if construction jobs, public or private, are to get done.[66] Fighting the practice may be ineffective or dangerous and is likely to delay work at considerable costs.[67] Knowing acquiescence is usually illegal and sometimes cowardly. Sorting out one's responsibilities in such cases may be difficult, but it seems safe to say that the obligation to oppose corruption increases with one's ability to do so.[68]

The moral problems caused by other people's sins are an old story. When one discovers the corruption of a friend or political ally, personal or political loyalties may conflict with legal duty or devotion to the public interest. The high value of loyalty in politics may make the conflict a wrenching one, but on principled grounds the sacrifice of law or public interest to loyalty in such a case can hardly be justified. There may be other ways to do right, however, than by blowing the whistle on a friend. A direct personal confrontation may serve both public interest and personal loyalty, if the corrupt practice can be ended and adequate restitution made.

B. Dilemmas of Choice

If policymakers sometimes have extraordinary obligations to defend a view of the public interest, it is also true that they have an ordinary duty to analyze the values at stake in all the issues with which they are concerned. Within their normal discretionary authority, which for many is quite broad, policymakers are charged with working for the public good.

Every action of a policymaker directed toward some good, toward some substantive or procedural value, is in a sense an ethical issue. Such relatively straightforward values as economic efficiency, however, pose difficult ethical problems only when choices must be made between values. Others, such as liberty, are harder to puzzle out. Disagreements occur about their meaning and their practical implications, as well as about how they should be prized in relation to other values.

Those in the field of public policy who spend time studying value conflicts have naturally been primarily concerned with these more complex values. Among them, they have emphasized environmental values, individual rights, equality, distributive justice, peace, and what have been called humane values, i.e., life itself and the quality of life.

These are the core values of the growing movement for increased ethical concerns in universities and in our national life. A special concern with these values is justified not only because of their intrinsic importance, but because they are values that appear to be threatened in our highly technological, bureaucratic, materially oriented, and somewhat depersonalized society. Policy courses in which these values play a central part seem further justified by their weakness in or absence from other aspects of the policy curriculum.

While this defense is persuasive, it may be too narrow. There are other complex values given little scope by our dominant styles of policymaking and policy analysis. The need for a more careful weighing of complex values—our central concern here— in fact cuts across the whole range of significant policy issues.

The dilemmas of choice, the problems of seeing and judging the moral stakes of policy, can be analyzed from two different points of view. One can begin with value conflicts as they are actually embodied in policy issues, or one can start by examining the ethical principles themselves.

The different approaches have largely similar aims. Both can counter tendencies to ignore some values and to oversimplify others, and both can lead to a fuller understanding of the ways in which moral reasoning can influence policy.

1. Issues

The significant choices—the issues—faced by policymakers are almost always ethically complicated. Policymakers need to know what values are actually involved in their options, and to what extent they are involved. The first task of anyone who wants to promote the use of moral reasoning in the analysis of policy is to offer suggestions for sorting out the moral complexities. A short description of the role of moral reasoning in policymaking is, however, a necessary preliminary here.

In the policy process, explicit debate about better and worse, or right and wrong, ordinarily occurs when objectives are formulated in relation to problems that are to be solved, and when alternative ways of achieving those objectives are arrayed for decision. Choices are not made directly between values, but rather between options that differ in the extent to which they embody particular values, or in the emphasis some values receive in relation to others.

To this rather conventional view certain qualifications should be added: values are also important at other stages of the policy process; debate about the ethical implications of choice ought not to be limited only to the marginal differences of value by which the chief available options differ; moral reasoning and debate affect how values are understood, so that they cannot be adequately treated as preferences or as analytic constraints. Each of these assertions runs counter to some of the implicit assumptions of policy analysis, and each has important consequences for understanding the role of ethical reasoning in policy choice.

Values shape the way problems are perceived; they are crucial to our notion that something is a problem to be solved, rather than a condition to be accepted. If the policy process begins in the recognition of a problem—in the view that something ought to be done—it begins with a moral assertion. Nor are values irrelevant to the other end of the policy process. After the normative tasks of setting out objectives and ranking options have been completed, the decisions that are made must be put into effect. The values of those who actively implement decisions can affect powerfully the actual shape of the ultimate policy.

If normative argument is pursued consciously only at the stage where objectives are set and alternatives fashioned, then it is hostage to unexamined values or to personal and organizational self-interest unopposed by critical moral reasoning.

Analysis cannot go on forever, and it would be thrifty to expend time and energy on the moral implications of a choice to be analyzed only to the extent that options faced by a decision-maker differ in the values they embody. But such an approach is unacceptably parsimonious. It is not only important to choose the best available option; it is also valuable to consider what might be a better choice even if it is not possible now, and to weigh carefully the larger costs of choice even when better options are unavailable. We intend no chimerical quest for comprehensive rationality. Moral reasoning cannot be carried on indefinitely, but it should not be restricted by claims that all the options have already been discovered. Critical analysis may, after all, generate new and less costly possibilities; and it may also, by emphasizing the costs of choice, serve to identify threatened values that merit the special concern of policymakers in relation to other issues.

The third of our assertions about values in the policy process was that values are changed as we reason about them, and that our language needs to reflect this understanding. Values refer to judgments about the common good as well as to conclusions about personal needs and desires. Our moral judgments may change when we see our intentions actually or imaginatively embodied in action. What we believe may also change when we find our ideas are inconsistent with one another, that our policies lack logical coherence, or that their foundations in factual reality are inadequate.

This is the common pattern of moral thinking and debate. While admissions of outright error are predictably rare, illogicality and the review of actual and probable consequences lead regularly to the alteration and adjustment of our values. Civil liberties or social equity or any other value may continue to be strongly held, but their meanings and applications may be refined or redirected.

All of this amounts to a picture of moral reasoning about policy that is far from Bentham's felicific calculus. Serious weighing of the moral stakes of policy takes time, as well as sensitivity to the whole range of values that may be involved in a decision. To the charge that such weighing will sometimes delay action, only a partial apology is offered. The need for promptness may indeed at times be great; and the values served by decisive action may sometimes be the most important values. But this case must be made. Haste is only a means; it has no intrinsic superiority to more deliberate speed.

To illuminate the moral complexities of policy choice, political theory, and writings by social scientists and historians that are informed by the traditional concerns of political theory are likely to be especially helpful. Political ideology, the shorthand of social philosophy, can also be of great value in calling attention to neglected values, and in taking account of dimensions of values that might otherwise be neglected. Legal argument can often be useful in identifying and resolving important aspects of moral choice. A great many ethical issues in American life eventually become constitutional questions, either because the Constitution is thought to express an agreed, if limited, hierarchy of values against which various normative claims may be tested, or because, lacking substantive agreement, the parties rely on procedural rules to settle their disputes.

Analyzing the values at stake in an issue is hardly ever a purely individual task. Much of the time policymakers are occupied with the adjudication of arguments, testing the logic and the coherence of the views that come before them. Policymakers, unlike philosophers, have a need to be sensitive to badly argued and even illogical positions. Desiring to know what is at stake, they have the task of finding or reconstructing as many cogent arguments about the public good involved in a choice as possible. They need especially to hear or to discover values responsive to the fears and hostilities of the least logical participants in debate. Only by doing so can they hope to extend participation or to build confidence in the integrity of the system or in their own fairness as decisionmakers.

When moral arguments about the issues are heard clearly, and values understood in an adequately complex fashion, areas of unresolved conflict about the public good clarify their shapes, but some conflicts, like the dispute about abortion, will be philosophically unresolvable. Here it is the task of ethical reasoning to elucidate ways of achieving decisions or of managing enduring conflict that will best maintain the whole range of values prized by a society.

A comprehensive catalog of values would be of little use in portraying the ethical complexities of policy choice. A diverse listing of generally neglected values might be more to the point, but it should be admitted that most of the values relevant to a policy choice will in one way or another be raised by partisans and analysts. A more important problem is to see adequately the particular dimensions of the broad values that are thought relevant to decisions.

In the relatively abbreviated comments that follow, several areas are identified in which complex moral reasoning seems more the exception than the rule. This partial list may be sufficiently suggestive to illustrate some of the kinds of thinking we believe are needed.

a. Environmental values

It would not be accurate to say that environmental values are on the whole neglected by students of policy or by governmental decisionmakers. Yet the public debate over these values is often inadequate, at least partly because of the unusually diverse range of principles and attitudes that are packed into the notion of environmental values.

Water pollution, for example, is variously attacked as dangerous to health and life, now or in the future; as uneconomic in the long run; as unesthetic—harmful to possibilities for recreation, or simply ugly; or as violative of certain moral principles arising out of our obligation to nature. These must be examined independently if we are to form any clear idea of how the costs of pollution may be compared with the costs of abatement, costs more easily measurable in higher prices or taxes, or in increased government regulation.

It is evident that disaggregating environmental values poses problems for which cost-benefit analysis is not an adequate tool. Nonutilitarian bases are urged for the defense of the environment from irreversible damage. It is argued on theological grounds, for example, that man has no right to such self-serving environmental manipulation. A similar case is made, absent a theological postulate, by giving some measure of moral authority to the natural world.[69] These nonutilitarian views may lead only to unresolvable disputes with philosophic opponents, but it is possible that examining them would reveal limits to a policymaker's knowledge or generate helpful guides to policy choice. The case for the moral authority of nature might, on reflection, lead someone who does not accept it to the discovery of a psychologically grounded case for environmental caution. We might, that is to say, have good psychological grounds for being careful of the natural world in which humankind developed and which we experience as a beneficent presence in our lives.

The old religious languages may have much to teach us about

moral choice even when their premises are the subject of dispute. Responsibility for future generations has often been a religious imperative, and it is one that may be defended on other grounds as well. Ancient demands for awe and humility before God's creation likewise need to be pondered even by policymakers whose world view is entirely secular. It seems appropriate that the head of New York City's Bureau of Radiation Control has adopted as a motto Lao Tse's proverb: "When men lack a sense of awe, there will be disaster."[70]

b. Extreme circumstances

Most of the time policymakers face or perceive relatively short-term problems. Little time is spent worrying about such fundamental questions as the legitimacy of the government or the long-term coherence of policy and civic life. Ordinarily, such a course is defensible and appropriate. Few decisions are likely to have profound effects on how citizens make sense of or relate to their political world. The problem is to be ready for the issues of fundamental importance when they appear, to recognize them and respond to them before they become acute. Policymakers need to sense the potential for alienation and even disloyalty that can arise out of the failure to satisfy any strongly felt demands; and they need to recognize how quickly bureaucratic indifference or perceived procedural unfairness can magnify that disaffection.

The consequences may be severe if even a small portion of the population comes to disbelieve in the legitimacy of the regime. When only a very few are willing to support terrorist acts, a whole society can face the convulsions of violence. The nightmare of Northern Ireland is only one of the hideous lessons available. Even without rebellion the costs of political disaffection may be severe. The processes whereby demands are articulated may atrophy, and segments of the citizenry may suffer from unmet needs. Nor should it be forgotten that the loss of loyalty is in itself a heavy cost, one that tends to weaken a sense of personal efficacy and to undermine the possibility of communal satisfactions.

c. Life and death

Much public policy is aimed at avoiding early or needless death, and it is tempting to see life as an absolute standard by which the costs and benefits of various such policies can be compared.[71] The application of this standard may reveal anomalies—life-saving equipment in a hospital may require large amounts of money spent per life saved, although more lives could be saved from the same amount of funds expended instead on highway safety. Does the anomaly call for reform?

As such issues are debated it is again important to think carefully about the values in question. Is it right that the identifiable lives of kidney-disease victims needing expensive dialysis receive greater public support than the unidentified but statistically predictable lives of those who will die from hitting fixed road signs at high speeds? It might be. The loss of known lives simply because money is lacking seems callous, and it tortures with guilt and regret the families and individuals who might have earned or saved enough to make survival possible. Moral reasoning about this subject might go much further. Protecting individuals from death by randomly acquired and slow terminal kidney disease may be thought more important than saving individuals from quick deaths for which their own choices are partly to blame. Arguments are rightly made that more money should be spent to avoid highway deaths, but it is not merely the political power of affected families that creates unwillingness to trade a few expensively preserved lives of kidney patients for a larger number of lives of traffic accident victims, more cheaply spared.

Saving lives is morally complicated in other ways as well. In the long run death can only be delayed, but we may all hope to postpone its dominion over our minds and choices. Vastly increased emphasis on health and the postponement of death might enthrall us, sapping our courage to face life, and prompting us to sacrifice concerns for quality and heightened consciousness in a beggarly quest for time.[72]

2. Principles

Since policy choices are often to be justified on the basis of coherent or even systematic principled positions, it follows that those positions themselves are the third major area in which ethical dilemmas may be expected to face those who make policy. To analyze these dilemmas is to raise many of the traditional questions of political philosophy. Much of what was said in the previous section bears on the subject of principled argument, but here a somewhat different focus is appropriate. Philosophical arguments themselves are the primary concern here, with applications and issues playing a secondary role.

In the previous sections we tried to show how philosophic and theoretical arguments might make clearer the values and responsibilities at stake in the acts and choices of policymakers. At this point we want to show something of how the study of those arguments, in depth and on their own terms, might contribute to the recognition and the resolution of the moral problems of policy choice.

The meaning of some of the great principles of our politics is changeable; notions like democracy or liberty are always subject to debate. Yet the way these principles are understood is a great and often determinative influence on policy. While a good background in political theory may help one to perceive the moral dimensions of many issues, there are some policy problems facing decisionmakers that can hardly be resolved without considerable theoretical analysis.

It would be tempting to comment in detail on some of the philosophic questions of greatest significance for policymakers. Opposing ideas of democracy,[73] the debates over negative and positive liberty,[74] and the related arguments about morality and the law[75] are subjects of great theoretical interest and considerable practical relevance to the choices of policymakers. Here we can do no more than suggest the beginnings of the case we would make for the study of such philosophic issues by commenting briefly in three important areas.

a. Justice

The most extensive and in some ways the most significant arguments about political philosophy in recent years have centered around the meaning of justice—the "first virtue of social institutions" as John Rawls, a principal figure in this discussion, has aptly called it.[76] These arguments have opposed contractarian notions to utilitarian ideas, with Rawls and some others holding that an adequate theory of justice is ultimately irreconcilable with utilitarianism.[77]

This lively debate about both the meaning of fairness and the patterns of the distribution of goods and services in our society has not been without consequences for policymaking. Affirmative action generally, and in particular the question of minority admissions quotas in education, have been discussed extensively against the background of the various theories of justice that have been advanced. In other areas, too, it is increasingly common to hear the needs and aspirations of citizens who are economically worst off defended in terms that owe much to this argument.

Anyone concerned with public policy needs to think seriously about justice and to recognize changes in the ideas about justice that are accepted by those who are politically active. The charge of injustice is always a serious one, and, if it can be sustained, may be argument enough to overturn a policy or to bring down a regime or to upend a social order.

b. Utility

It is hardly fair to say that the typical policymaker has consciously adopted utilitarianism as a moral philosophy, or that he or she is prepared to defend this or that variant of the doctrine.[78] Yet formulations like "the greatest good for the greatest number" have long been the *lingua franca* of normative discourse in Washington, and in the state houses and city halls as well. Beyond this, the principle of utility has great force in its guise of efficiency, the objective toward which economic analysis is geared.

As it is commonly understood in America, utility refers to social happiness, based on the states of mind of the individuals who make up society. Happiness consists in pleasures attained and pains avoided, and even if all of these are not in the strictest sense calculable, it is generally believed that all are in principle commensurable. While the view that preferences revealed in a free market—political as well as economic—can serve as a proxy for the hedonistic calculus is challenged in many quarters, the underlying principle that each person is the only proper judge of his or her individual pleasure is broadly held.

As a guide for policy, the principle of utility has its internal limitations. Our knowledge of states of mind is necessarily indirect for all but ourselves, and preferences, however revealed, are only an approximate guide to happiness or utility. Moreover, preferences are available only in relation to alternatives individuals know, and may vary as knowledge deepens and spreads. A much more serious internal problem is the necessity for rather arbitrary decisions about which methods will be used for aggregating preferences.[79]

The principle of utility is an important part of our moral thinking, whatever its internal problems. Because it is, the diverse and sometimes contradictory implications bound up in it need sorting out. Some acquaintance with the plurality of utilitarian thought may help decisionmakers to ask more clearly: whose benefits? measured in what fashion? and compared to others on what basis? A familiarity with rule-utilitarianism can raise questions about the conclusions of consequential calculations when these run counter to existing laws or settled principles.

Policymakers should be aware as well that utilitarian calculation can become a habit that obscures important moral realities. The need for commensurability can tend to give extra weight to the more easily quantified dimensions of a problem, leaving aside or undervaluing considerations of honor or beauty or anguish or unfairness.[80] Utilitarianism's general difficulty in satisfactorily accounting for our experience of rules and obligation, and more particularly the obligation to keep promises,[81] is another limitation that should emphasize the need to employ moral reasoning that goes beyond the principle of utility.

c. Community

The somewhat inchoate language of community adopted by many young people in the 1960s was disturbing, even frightening, for many of those who lived through the nightmare of European fascism. They remembered that Hitler's idea of the *volksgemeinschaft*, the community of all the people, had spoken powerfully to an earlier generation somehow alienated from the triumphs of modernity. When direct action politics became more turbulent, and when violence was tolerated or advocated by some, the fears grew mightily. There was, however, little Hitlerian about the communitarianism of the counterculture.

The joys of solidarity, of community and fraternity, of politics itself,[82] are for other reasons as well somewhat suspect among those who write about politics. The first of these is that such joys represent "irrational" enthusiasm, outside the calculations of the interested self.[83] More important, perhaps, communitarian notions are feared because they are almost inevitably limited or parochial in their reach. Ethnic solidarity is purchased at the price of distinctness; neighborhood unity is a bulwark of residential segregation; fraternal organizations seem dedicated to upholding the ethnocentric, sometimes racist ideals of a bygone era.

Yet we would want to insist on the great value of solidarity with others. It may be attached to other values and attitudes we reject. But when policy militates against community, even for the most decent reasons, the cost needs to be felt and felt keenly. What we prize involves feelings that seem to us supportive of personal strength and of generosity to others. Not all forms of social unity are rightly called community. We would, for example, distinguish a calculated "self-seeking in company"[84] from the emotionally deeper experience of community.

The rhetoric of community often suggests that every aspect of modern social life tends to its destruction. That is clearly a delusion. Long-term association of neighbors may be less likely in an age of rapid geographical mobility, but planes and cars and telephones make it far more possible than ever to maintain close ties with chosen friends living at a distance. For those whose community is by choice and conscious intent, and perhaps for those who prize intensity and liveliness of interaction over permanence, it may even seem an age of rich communal possibility.

These reflections on community are relevant to policy in several areas. At the most obvious level, it may be observed that had the value of community been more highly prized, housing and highway planners would have been more inhibited in their wanton destruction of traditional communities. Beyond this, the effects of welfare, education, and employment policies in maintaining or weakening communal ties might be more regularly considered were attention directed to the idea of community.

The New Deal's communitarian programs in agriculture—some of America's most remarkable and least known social experiments[85]—were ultimately destroyed by the partisans of more conventional views. In the 1960s, independent communalism received no governmental help. National and regional cooperativism supportive of communal values has yet to gain any serious or long-term encouragement from federal agencies. The possibilities inherent in nontraditional communities are being explored by individuals, but any opportunities for governmental encouragement seem almost entirely to have escaped the attention of those responsible for shaping our institutions.

3. The uses of theory

Moral reasoning extends from our worst fears to our finest hopes. Thinking about the two extremes is a primary obligation of the theorist. Theory is powerfully critical of society when it sets forth ideals and fashions possibilities for human action. Less obviously, perhaps, theoretical investigation is critical when it attempts to penetrate the screen of apparent reality to reveal unknown underlying stresses and patterns of disorder or decay.

In weighing our fears, the task of the theorist is, as Hannah Arendt once put it, to see the social order falling apart.[86] The intention is not predictive, estimating the future in ways the facts can be expected to confirm; it is prophetic, identifying future possibilities in the hope that they can be avoided by sounding an alarm in time. Theoretical investigation is concerned with legitimacy and with disputes that might grow to conflict or violence, or to threaten the order as a whole.

Another way of describing what theorists do is to say that they are concerned primarily with what we don't know. Employing ways of reasoning alternative to ordinary patterns of political analysis, they search for insights that might reveal neglected values or opportunities.

The traditions of philosophy and political theory offer a great many modes of thinking that may be fruitful for creative work on policy problems. Dialectical modes of reasoning and ordinary language philosophy, to choose only two examples, have each been used in recent years by students of politics to justify claims of importance to policymakers and to generate new insights about politics.[87]

One cannot know everything or master several disciplines, but it seems very wise for at least some of those involved in policymaking to know a good bit of theory. Theoretical investigation begins, after all, with our ignorance, and it insists that the world is, as Sheldon Wolin has claimed, richer and fuller than any of the things we say about it.[88] That perspective may be an indispensable corrective for the hubris almost unavoidably engendered by the increasingly impressive techniques of rational analysis available to those who study policy.

Notes

1. Of 219 schools and programs in public policy and public administration, 134 responded to our letter, sent in the fall of 1978. Of these, 77 reported that no ethics program existed, while 26 indicated a required course of ethics, and 32 reported one or more optional courses. Of the total 72 courses reported, the majority seem principally concerned with dilemmas of responsibility faced by individual decisionmakers (see part III–A of our paper) and with policy issues involving conflicting values (part III–B:1). Only a minority, 27 by our count, make any substantial use of materials written by philosophers and political theorists.

A full tabulation of the results of the survey, including course titles and instructors, is available from the authors upon request.

2. There are far fewer undergraduate than graduate programs in policy—among the policy schools only Duke and Princeton offer a full undergraduate major—but our impression is that ethics may play a greater role in the education of undergraduate policy students. Where courses in ethics and policy are available as electives, undergraduates may have considerably more opportunity to fit them into their schedules without paying a price in foregone instruction about analytic techniques.

3. Edith Stokey and Richard Zeckhauser, *A Primer for Policy Analysis* (New York: Norton, 1978), pp. 134f.

4. Ibid., pp. 277–86, "In sum, we believe that government participation in the resource allocation processes of society can be justified on two grounds only: 1. *Equity:* A more desirable distribution of goods and services among the members of the society is fostered. 2. *Efficiency:* Efficiency is promoted in situations where the market has failed."

5. Ibid., p. 283.

6. Vernon Van Dyke, *Political Science: A Philosophical Analysis* (Stanford, Calif.: Stanford University Press, 1960), p. 12.

7. So Milton Friedman evidently believes: he refers to "...fundamental differences in basic values, differences about which men can ultimately only fight." Quoted in Stokey and Zeckhauser, *A Primer....*, p. 261.

8. Charles E. Lindblom, "The Science of Muddling Through," in *Public Administration,* ed. Robert T. Golembiewski et al (Chicago: Rand McNally, 1966), p. 298.

9. *The Teaching of Ethics in Higher Education: A Report by The Hastings Center* (Hastings-on-Hudson, N.Y.: The Hastings Center, 1980), pp. 82–83.

10. Ibid., pp. 58–62, 81.

11. Ibid., pp. 48–52, 80.

12. Ibid., p. 64.

13. John Rohr's valuable new book, *Ethics for Bureaucrats* (New York: Dekker, 1978), shows something of the importance of legal principles and legal argument in this field.

14. A good example of a decision involving all three types of moral dilemma is Lincoln's policy toward slavery in 1862. Temporizing, Lincoln offered his antislavery critics the argument that maintaining the union was his *"official* duty," to be pursued, if necessary, even at the expense of his "oft-expressed *personal* wish that all men everywhere could be free." (Italics in original). The claim that official duty must supersede personal wish would be difficult to deny, but as Lincoln knew, the issue was hardly so simple. His opponents held the view that the extirpation of slavery was a moral duty, and some believed that duty superior to the Constitution, while Lincoln had himself earlier taken the position that liberty for all was an essential aspect of the Union.

In fact, Lincoln faced uncertainties at all three levels: his acceptance of the oath of office seemed to impose special duties for the maintenance of the Union, and duties only the president could fulfill; the effects on slavery and on the war of immediate emancipation, or of delays of varying lengths, were difficult to estimate or to value comparatively; and the relative importance of freedom for slaves as against peace or national unity was not, for Lincoln, entirely clear. See *Abraham Lincoln: Selected Speeches, Messages and Letters,* ed. T. Harry Williams (New York: Rinehart, 1958), "Letter to Horace Greeley," pp. 190f.; and Stephen B. Oates, *With Malice Toward None: The Life of Abraham Lincoln* (New York: Harper & Row, 1977), pp. 267–70, 297ff., 307–13.

15. Graham Allison, *The Essence of Decision: Explaining the Cuban Missile Crisis* (Boston: Little, Brown, 1971), pp. 252–55 and passim.

16. Robert Art offers a valuable critique of some of Allison's assumptions in "Bureaucratic Politics and American Foreign Policy," *Policy Sciences* 4 (1973), 467–90.

17. See J. Roland Pennock's thoughtful essay, "The Problem of Responsibility," in Carl J. Friedrich ed., *Responsibility: Nomos III* (New York: The Liberal Arts Press, 1960), pp. 3–27.

18. Paul A. Freund, "Social Justice and the Law," in *On Law and Social Justice* (Cambridge, Mass.: Harvard University Press, 1968), p. 85. Cf. John Rawls: "Justice is the first virtue of social institutions, as truth is of systems of thought." *A Theory of Justice* (Cambridge, Mass.: Harvard University Press, 1971), p. 3. Advanced in support of a conception of justice almost wholly distributional, Rawls's analogy may be too restrictive. By seeing justice in relation to norms of community and authority, as well as the distributive norm of equality, Freund's analysis in "Social Justice and the Law" makes the problem of justice more complicated and, at the same time, makes imaginable a greater variety of potentially just regimes.

19. Consider Lon Fuller's helpful distinction between the "morality of duty" and the "morality of aspiration" in *The Morality of Law* (New Haven: Yale University Press, 1964), chap. 1, "The Two Moralities." Sin, as viewed by a morality of aspiration, is "a failure in the effort to achieve a realization of the human quality of life itself." Ibid., p. 3. The subject of the moral qualities needed by public officials is discussed in Stephen K. Bailey's "Ethics and the Public Service," *Public Administration Review* 24 (December, 1964), 234–43.

20. Cf. Glendon Schubert, "Is There a Public Interest Theory?" and Frank J. Sorauf, "The Conceptual Muddle," in *The Public Interest: Nomos V*, ed. Carl J. Friedrich (New York: Atherton, 1962), pp. 162–76, 183–90.

21. The most impressive of these is Richard Flathman's *The Public Interest: An Essay Concerning the Normative Discourse of Politics* (New York: Wiley, 1966). See also Brian Barry "The Public Interest," in *Proceedings of the Aristotelian Society*, suppl. vol. 38 (1964), and Virginia Held, *The Public Interest and Individual Interests* (New York: Basic Books, 1970).

22. For an able exposition of ways in which ordinary language philosophy can be used in the analysis of the concepts of political theory see the Introduction to *Concepts in Social and Political Philosophy* (New York: Macmillan, 1973) by Richard Flathman.

23. E.g., Arthur Maass, *Muddy Waters: The Army Engineers and the Nation's* (Cambridge: Harvard University Press, 1951) "Gauging Administrative Responsibility," discussed in Herbert Spiro, *Responsibility in Government: Theory and Practice* (New York: Van Nostrand, 1969), pp. 83–105.

24. Herbert Simon, *Administrative Behavior* (New York: Macmillan, 1947), pp. 45–60.

25. Wayne Leys, "Platonic, Pragmatic, and Political Responsibility," in *Responsibility...*, ed. Carl J. Friedrich, p. 79.

26. Even in war. "Morality in war is not settled by any single measure; it is a matter of long-term agreements and precedents as much or more than of immediate arithmetic....War is only a temporary rupture in international society and...it is a recurrent rupture. For both these reasons, it ought never to be a total rupture." Michael Walzer "Moral Judgment in Time of War," in *War and Morality*, ed. Richard Wasserstrom (Belmont, Calif.: Wadsworth, 1970), p. 62.

27. Robert Dallek, *Franklin D. Roosevelt and American Foreign Policy, 1932–1945* (New York: Oxford University Press, 1979), p. 250. See Sissela Bok's excellent discussion of Johnson and Roosevelt in *Lying: Moral Choice in Public Life* (New York: Pantheon Books, 1978), pp. 170–81. A somewhat more favorable view of FDR's deception is evident in Wilson Carey McWilliam's "Honesty and Political Authority," in *The Right to Know, to Withhold, and to Lie*, ed. William J. Barnds (New York: The Council on Religion and International Affairs, 1969). Dallek's book offers a good basis for making judgments about this controversy. In FDR's defense, it should be pointed out that his promise—although knowingly deceptive—nevertheless inhibited his actions throughout the succeeding thirteen months. Until Pearl Harbor, Roosevelt was less willing than he might otherwise have been to push the country into confrontations with the Axis powers.

28. James Fenton, "Against Honesty," *New Statesman*, 23 August 1974, p. 252. The qualification is owed to Bok, *Lying...*, p. 178.

29. "...Power, by its very nature, can never produce a substitute for the secure stability of factual reality, which, because it is past, has grown into a dimension beyond our reach." Hannah Arendt, "Truth and Politics," in *Between Past and Future* (Baltimore: Penguin, 1977), p. 258.

30. David Halberstam, *The Best and the Brightest* (New York: Random House, 1972), p. 581.

31. Bok notes that even lies only to liars are not easily justified when the relevant arguments and considerations are examined. *Lying...*, chap. 9, pp. 123–33.

32. Alistair Horne, *A Savage War of Peace: Algeria 1954–1962* (New York: Viking, 1978), pp. 377–81, 457.

33. Ibid., pp. 442–537.

34. Lincoln Steffens, *Autobiography* (New York: Harcourt, Brace 1931), p. 774.

35. Harry McPherson relates a possibly apocryphal story about Alben Barkley. "...Barkley was interrupted in the middle of a magnificent town square speech in Eastern Kentucky when someone yelled, 'How do you stand on FEPC?' Barkley surveyed the crowd. Eastern Kentucky, like Eastern Tennessee, had long been divided on the racial issue. There were the grandchildren of Unionists and of Confederates and Copperheads in that audience; no one knew how many of each. At last Barkley quietly replied, 'I'm all right on FEPC.' And went on with his speech." *A Political Education* (Boston: Atlantic-Little, Brown, 1972), p. 66.

36. Bok, *Lying...*, pp. 158–64. A recent and persuasive account of the crucial issues at stake is A. Kenneth Pye, "The Role of Counsel in the Suppression of Truth," *Duke Law Journal* 4 (October 1978) 921–59.

37. Halberstam, *The Best...*, p. 603–10.

38. Editors of *The Washington Post* have said that more than 50 percent of the documents leaked anonymously to their paper are never written about at all. (Interviews with Eugene H. Patterson (1972) and Haynes Johnson (1978), B. L. P.)

39. William Manchester, *American Caesar: Douglas MacArthur 1880–1964* (Boston: Little, Brown, 1978), p. 429. See also pp. 368–72.

40. Ibid., pp. 629–44. Manchester's version of these events is inadequate. See Forrest Pogue's careful criticisms in his review of *American Caesar,* "The Military in a Democracy," *International Security* 3, no. 4 (Spring 1979), 59–79. Pogue's well-reasoned verdict on MacArthur in the 1951 crisis, pp. 75–79, is considerably harsher than Manchester's.

41. The best account is in Robert J. Donovan's *Conflict and Crisis: The Presidency of Harry S. Truman, 1945–1948* (New York: Norton, 1977), pp. 219–28. Truman's own account was less than candid, but it has its moments: "Well I had to fire Henry today, and of course I hated to do it. Henry Wallace is the best Secretary of Agriculture this country ever had....Well, now he's out, and the crackpots are having conniption fits. I'm glad they are. It convinces me I'm right..." *Memoirs* vol. 1, *Year of Decisions* (Garden City, N.Y.: Doubleday, 1955), p. 560.

42. Secretary of War Stimson was clearly uneasy about his role in the Japanese internment (he worked consistently to improve the conditions of the camps), but he defended what was done: "What the critics ignored was the situation that led to the evacuation. Japanese raids on the West Coast seemed not only possible but probable in the first months of the war, and it was quite impossible to be sure that the raiders would not receive help from individuals of Japanese origin. More than that, anti-Japanese feelings on the Coast had reached a level which endangered the lives of all such individuals." Henry L. Stimson and McGeorge Bundy, *On Active Service in Peace and War* (New York: Harper, 1948), p. 406.

As far as national security goes, it is clear that this is an excuse, not a justification. Pearl Harbor *seemed* then to make the risk a plausible one, although U-boats off the East Coast did not put German-Americans under similar suspicion. Stimson's own judgment might have been otherwise but for a somewhat paternalistic solicitude for the Japanese-Americans and a not very brave capitulation to racist California hysteria.

It is worth noting that one of the figures fostering the hysteria was California Attorney General Earl Warren, who was preparing to run for governor. Earl Warren, *Memoirs* (Garden City, N.Y.: Doubleday, 1977), p. 107. Warren's later regret was deep, and he came to regard the decision as mistaken. It may be that this untypical failing helped to solidify and give force to his long-standing concern for the rights of minorities.

43. Maeva Marcus, *Truman and the Steel Seizure Case: The Limits of Presidential Power* (New York: Columbia University Press, 1977), pp. 195–227 and passim.

44. M. Nelson McGeary, *Gifford Pinchot* (Princeton, N.J.: Princeton University Press, 1960), p. 158. Interestingly enough, Pinchot's friend and sometime lawyer, Henry Stimson, had a hand in drafting the letter.

45. Ibid., p. 129. Pinchot went on to say: "An institution or a law is a means, not an end, a means to be used for the public good, to be modified for the public good, and to be interpreted for the public good....The people, not the law, should have every benefit of the doubt."

46. Pinchot and Teddy Roosevelt himself had earlier violated the intentions of Congress, while staying within the law, by withdrawing millions of acres of forest reserves from the public lands and placing them under Forest Service control. Working continuously for ten days while a bill to prohibit such withdrawals lay on the President's desk, the new forests were approved and announced just before the bill was signed.

47. Ibid., pp. 116–17.

48. Mortimer R. Kadish and Sanford H. Kadish, *Discretion to Disobey: A Study of Lawful Departures from Legal Rules* (Stanford, Calif.: Stanford University Press, 1973), pp. 93f. See also William Van Alstyne, "Congress, the President and the Power to Declare War: A Requiem for Vietnam," 121 *University of Pennsylvania Law Review* 1 (1972).

49. On this point, as on representation generally, Hannah Pitkin's insights and careful arguments are of the greatest value. Her book, *The Concept of Representation* (Berkeley: University of California Press, 1967), is the major and essential work in the field. Readers desiring a brief synoptic view will find very helpful her Introduction to *Representation*, ed. Hannah Fenichel Pitkin, (New York: Atherton Press, 1969).

50. Kenneth Culp Davis, *Discretionary Justice: A Preliminary Inquiry* (Baton Rouge: Louisiana State University Press, 1969), pp. 19–26.

51. Paul Appleby, *Morality and Administration in Democratic Government* (Baton Rouge: Louisiana State University Press, 1952) passim. Stephen K. Bailey, "Ethics and the Public Service," in *Public Administration Review* 24, pp. 234–37; Frederick C. Mosher, *Democracy and the Public Service* (New York: Oxford University Press, 1968), chap. 7, pp. 202–19.

52. Mosher, ibid., p. 212, summarizing Appleby.

53. Emmette S. Redford, *Democracy in the Administrative State* (New York: Oxford University Press, 1969), pp. 136–47.

54. In *Red Tape: Its Origins, Uses, and Abuses* (Washington, D.C.: Brookings Institution, 1977), Herbert Kaufman breaks a lance for procedural safeguards, noting that they arise from a concern with the rights of individuals in and out of government. Cf. the much more critical view of "red tape" taken by the Commission on Federal Paperwork in its final and summary report of October 3, 1977.

55. See Victor A. Thompson, *Without Sympathy or Enthusiasm: The Problem of Administrative Compassion* (University, Alabama: University of Alabama Press, 1975). In our view Thompson seriously underestimates the need for compassion and unjustifiably opposes it to fairness and rationality in administration. But his review of varying positions on the issues at stake is highly instructive.

56. An elegant and wide-ranging survey of advisory roles and problems is Herbert Goldhamer's *The Advisor* (New York: Elsevier, 1979).

57. See "What are Unions Doing to the Merit System?" by David T. Stanley, in *Conducting the People's Business,* ed. William G. Hills et al (Norman, Okla.: University of Oklahoma Press, 1973), pp. 453–60. A helpful bibliography follows this selection: ibid., pp. 461f. An important and extremely interesting recent addition to this literature is *Bureaucratic Insurgency: The Case of Police Unions* (Lexington, Mass.: Lexington Books, D.C. Heath, 1977) by Margaret Levi.

58. See Michael Walzer's "Political Action: The Problem of Dirty Hands," *Philosophy and Public Affairs* (Spring 1973), and the earlier writers on the question to whom he makes reference.

59. In this connection, we would question Walzer's willingness to tolerate a degree of corruption as the price of winning an election. Ibid., p. 166.

60. In July of 1889, Civil Service Commissioner Theodore Roosevelt held a hearing in Milwaukee on illegal patronage in post office hiring. There Roosevelt promised to protect the job of Hamilton Shidy, a postal employee who gave evidence against his superior of illegal appointments to post office jobs. When the Milwaukee postmaster fired Shidy, and Postmaster General Wanamaker, an opponent of reform, refused to intervene, Roosevelt faced a difficult choice: "As Shidy's protector, he was in honor bound to find him another federal job. But as Civil Service Commissioner, he was in honor bound to enforce the law. How could he give patronage to a confessed falsifier of government records? How could he, in all conscience, not do so?" TR chose to place Shidy in a patronage job at the Bureau of the Census. The upshot was a congressional investigation, and after a skillful and impassioned defense, a vindication of Roosevelt's reputation. See Edmund Morris, *The Rise of Theodore Roosevelt* (New York: Coward, McCann, 1979), pp. 403–6, 418–23, q. at 406.

In this case, resignation would not seem to be a reasonable way out of the dilemma, but two honorable courses, each possibly superior to the choice he made, were open to Roosevelt. He might have paid a reasonable sum—say, a year's salary for Shidy—to make up for the personal damages his rash promise caused. Alternatively, he might have secured private employment, or an indemnity, from any one of the wealthy partisans of civil service reform who were Roosevelt's friends and allies.

61. Albert O. Hirschman, *Exit, Voice, and Loyalty* (Cambridge Mass.: Harvard University Press, 1970). Brian Barry has argued that exit and voice are not

alternatives, that "exit-stay" and "voice-silence" are interdependent alternatives; *"Exit, Voice, and Loyalty:* a Review," *British Journal of Political Science* 4 (1974), 79–104. And see Michael Laver's thoughtful discussion of the notion of loyalty in "Cultural Aspects of Loyalty: On Hirschman and Loyalism in Ulster," *Political Studies* 24, no. 4, 469–77.

62. David Halberstam's account of the relationship between Michael Forrestal and John McNaughton suggests a few of the advantages and risks here; *The Best and the Brightest,* pp. 366–69. See also Halberstam's account of "Harriman's people," passim.

63. See Ronald Wraith and Edgar Simpkins, *Corruption in Developing Countries* (London: Allen and Unwin, 1963), and James C. Scott, *Comparative Political Corruption* (Englewood Cliffs, N.J.: Prentice-Hall, 1972). Professor Donald Warwick has called into question the tendency of some scholars to see such corrupt behavior in developing areas as "functional" or beneficial. We share his reservation, and we look forward to the publication of relevant material from his Indonesian studies. The argument that corrupt behavior played a helpful role in American development seems to us unproved and unlikely.

64. On the basis of logical inferences we find unconvincing, Edward Banfield offers a rather Spenglerian prognosis of increasing corruption in "Corruption as a Feature of Governmental Organization," *The Journal of Law and Economics* 28, no. 3 (December 1975), 587–605.

65. Mayor Lindsay faced such a dilemma in relation to policy corruption in New York City. His failure to respond to the revelations of Frank Serpico led ultimately to the investigations by the Knapp Commission. Revelations about corruption are news, and they can be expected whether or not they seem convenient to the person on top.

66. Commission to Investigate Allegations of Policy Corruption and the City's Anti-Corruption Procedures (Knapp Commission), *Commission Report,* pp. 123–31 "Corruption in the Construction Industry." Reprinted in *Theft of the City: Readings on Corruption in Urban America,* ed. John A. Gardiner and David J. Olson (Bloomington, Ind.: Indiana University Press, 1974), pp. 229–36.

67. The line between corruption and extortion is not always easy to draw— witness the 1972 Nixon campaign demands on regulated industries for illegal contributions.

68. Partly on this assumption, Robert Caro condemns Robert Moses in *The Power Broker* (New York: Alfred A. Knopf, 1974). Personally uncorrupt, Moses' vast operations were a cornucopia of illegal advantage for a wide variety of dishonest figures in politics, construction, and elsewhere.

69. See Stuart Hampshire, "Morality and Pessimism," *The New York Review of Books,* Jan. 25, 1973, p. 33; Laurence H. Tribe, "Ways Not to Think About Plastic & Trees," in *When Values Conflict: Essays on Environmental Analysis,*

Discourse, and Decisions, ed. Tribe et al (Cambridge, Mass.: Ballinger, 1976), pp. 83–88 and passim. James Griffin argues against this view in "Are There Incommensurable Values?" *Philosophy and Public Affairs* 7, no. 1, (1977), 39–59.

70. Fred C. Shapiro "Radiation Route," *The New Yorker,* November 13, 1978, p. 160. Cf. Lao Tse, *Tao Te Ching* trans. Gia-fu Feng and Jane English (New York: Vintage, 1972), chap. 72. Shapiro's discussion of the nuclear waste disposal problems of the Brookhaven research facility is one of the finest brief case studies available of a complicated conflict among values.

71. The literature on valuing lives is broad. A very interesting recent symposium is "Valuing Lives," *Law and Contemporary Problems* 40 no. 4 (Autumn 1976), ed. Philip Cook and James W. Vaupel. See also Richard Zeckhauser, "Procedures for Valuing Lives," *Public Policy* no. 23, (1975), 419 et seq.; and M. W. Jones-Lee, *The Value of Life: An Economic Analysis* (Chicago: The University of Chicago Press, 1976). On kidney disease, see Richard Rettig's contribution, "The Policy Debate on Patient Care Financing for Victims of End-Stage Renal Disease," to the Cook-Vaupel symposium, "Valuing Lives," pp. 196–230.

72. Jim Vaupel, in "Early Death: An American Tragedy," ibid., p. 116, cites Homer, *Iliad* I, lines 286–7, to the effect that early death is the "cruelest of destinies." This was, as he says, the view of Achilles' mother; but it may be worth noting that Achilles himself took a quite different position, dreading dishonor and even ordinariness less than glory, even with its risk of early death. In the *Odyssey* Achilles' shade seems to take a different view, XI, lines 490–505. Yet even here Achilles retains his joy and pride in the death-defying exploits of his son (lines 500–550).

73. One recent and important critique of conventional notions of democratic government, based on the belief that a genuinely democratic vision would require both cooperation and vastly more in the way of active citizenship, is Lawrence Goodwyn's excellent history of late nineteenth-century agrarian radicalism, *Democratic Promise: The Populist Moment in America* (New York: Oxford University Press, 1976).

74. See Isaiah Berlin, "Introduction" and "Two Concepts of Liberty," in *Four Essays on Liberty* (Oxford at the University Press, 1969); C. B. MacPherson, "Berlin's Division of Liberty," in *Democratic Theory: Essays in Retrieval* (Oxford: Clarendon Press, 1973), pp. 95–113; Gerald C. MacCallum Jr., "Negative and Positive Freedom," *Philosophical Review* 76 (1967), 312–34; Ronald Dworkin, "What Rights Do We Have," in *Taking Rights Seriously* (Cambridge, Mass.: Harvard University Press, 1978), pp. 266–78.

75. Patrick Devlin, *The Enforcement of Morals* (London: Oxford University Press, 1965); H. L. A. Hart, *Law Liberty and Morality* (Stanford, Calif.: Stanford University Press, 1963); Ronald Dworkin, "Liberty and Moralism," in *Taking Rights Seriously* pp. 240–58; Ernest Nagel, "The Enforcement of Mor-

als," *The Humanist* 208, no. 3 (May/June 1968) 20–27; Joel Feinberg, "Moral Enforcement and the Harm Principle," in *Social Philosophy* (Englewood Cliffs, N.J.: Prentice-Hall, 1973).

76. John Rawls, *A Theory of Justice* (Cambridge, Mass.: Harvard University Press, 1972).

77. See also Brian Barry's powerful critique of liberal theories of justice as taking inadequate account of collective goods. *The Liberal Theory of Justice* (Oxford: Clarendon Press, 1973), chap. 11.

78. William Frankena discusses act-, rule-, and general utilitarianism, noting that each category includes a family of views. *Ethics* (Englewood Cliffs, N.J.: Prentice-Hall, 1963), pp. 34–43.

79. A short and very clear description of some of these internal difficulties may be found in Lester Thurow, *Generating Inequality* (New York: Basic Books, 1975), pp. 33–43. Another clear and much fuller account is offered in chap. 13 of Stokey and Zeckhauser, *A Primer for Policy Analysis*. The latter account is confident that "satisfactory processes for social choice" (p. 284) can nevertheless be erected on a foundation of approximations based on welfare economics.

80. Stuart Hampshire's critique of utilitarianism in "Morality and Pessimism" raises these questions effectively. Hampshire argues that utilitarianism represented the cutting edge of social reform from the early nineteenth century until about World War II, but that it cannot now serve that function.

81. See A. I. Melden, "Utility and Moral Reasoning," *Ethics and Society*, ed. Richard T. De George (New York: Anchor Books, 1966), pp. 173–96.

82. See Wilson Carey McWilliams, *The Idea of Fraternity in America* (Berkeley: University of California Press, 1973), passim; and Hannah Arendt, *On Revolution* (New York: Viking, 1965), discussing "council government." A remarkable account of the extraordinary joys of revolutionary times is Aristide Zolberg's "Moments of Madness," *Politics and Society* 2, no. 2 (Winter 1972), 183–207.

83. Albert O. Hirschman, in *The Passions and the Interests: Political Arguments for Capitalism before Its Triumph* (Princeton, N.J.: Princeton University Press, 1977), gracefully lays out the origins of this view.

84. Betrand de Jouvenel, *The Pure Theory of Politics* (Cambridge: Cambridge University Press, 1963), p. 66. "But the better the thing, the worse its caricature. The community which arises out of love or friendship cannot be contrived by decree, the intensive emotions which it is proposed to extend wear thin. Such is our hankering for union with our fellows that the less we achieve it in our daily commerce, the more we dream of 'instituting' it at large—a dream which has proved to generate hate more often than harmony. Also, the network of well-wishers,which naturally fosters the happiness of Ego, if used by him in furtherance of some eagerly sought prize, changes in character. The

prize-seeker had better recruit a coalition on the basis of common interests or a shared passion, or a spoils-sharing covenant. Then, however, there is no one-to-one linking, but a banding together: this is self-seeking in company."

85. David Price, "The 'Quest for Community' in Public Policy," A Poynter Center Essay (1977), pp. 3–8.

86. Speaking at Union Theological Seminary at the thirtieth anniversary celebration of *Christianity and Crisis.*

87. Richard J. Bernstein, *The Restructuring of Social and Political Theory* (University of Pennsylvania Press, 1976), see esp. "The Critical Theory of Society," pp. 171–236; Hanna Fenichel Pitkin, *Wittgenstein and Justice: On the Significance of Ludwig Wittgenstein for Social and Political Thought* (Berkeley: University of California Press, 1972).

88. Sheldon Wolin, "Political Theory as a Vocation," *American Political Science Review* 63 (1969) 1073.

Bibliography

I. Ethics in the Policy Curriculum

Brown, Peter. "Ethics and Policy: A Preliminary Analysis," *Policy Studies Journal* 7 (Autumn 1978): 132–37.

Callahan, Daniel and Bok, Sissela, eds. *Ethics Teaching in Higher Education.* New York: Plenum Press, 1980.

The Teaching of Ethics in Higher Education: A Report by The Hastings Center. Hastings-on-Hudson, N.Y.: The Hastings Center, 1980.

Dolbeare, Kenneth M. "Public Policy Analysis and the Coming Struggle for the Soul of the Postbehavioral Revolution." In *Power and Community.* Edited by Philip Green and Sanford Levinson. New York: Random House, 1970.

Jonson, A. R. and Butler, L. H. "Public Ethics and Policymaking," *Hastings Center Report* 5, no. 4 (August 1975).

Kaplan, Abraham. "American Ethics and Public Policy." In *The American Style: Essays in Value and Performance.* Edited by Elting E. Morison. New York: Harper & Brothers, 1958.

MacRae, Duncan, Jr. "Scientific Communication, Ethical Argument, and Public Policy," *American Political Science Review* 65, no. 1 (March 1971).

Price, David E. "Public Policy and Ethics," in *Hastings Center Report* 7, no. 6, Special Supplement (December 1977): 4–6.

Reid, Herbert G. and Ernest J. Yanarella. "Political Science and the Post-Modern Critique of Scientism and Domination." *The Review of Politics* 37, no. 3 (July 1975).

Rein, Martin. *Social Science and Public Policy.* New York: Penguin Books, 1976.

Rohr, John A. *Ethics for Bureaucrats*. New York: Dekker, 1978.

―――. "Reflections on Ethics and Management Training." *Good Government* 99, (Summer 1976): 7–11.

Self, Peter. *Econocrats and the Policy Process: The Politics and Philosophy of Cost-Benefit Analysis*. London: Macmillan Ltd., 1975.

―――. "The Study of Ethics in the Political Science Curriculum." *Public Administration Review* 36, no. 4 (July/August, 1976).

Tribe, Laurence H. "Policy Science: Analysis or Ideology." *Philosophy and Public Affairs* 2, no. 1 (Fall 1972): pp. 66–113.

Wildavsky, Aaron. "Rescuing Policy Analysis from PPBS." In *Public Expenditures and Policy Analysis*. Edited by Robert H. Haveman and Julius Margolis. Chicago: Markham, 1970.

II. Dilemmas of Responsibility

Appleby, Paul H. *Morality and Administration in Democratic Government*. Baton Rouge: Louisiana State University Press, 1952.

Arendt, Hannah. "Lying in Politics." In *Crises of the Republic*. New York: Harcourt Brace Jovanovich, 1972.

Bailey, Stephen. "Ethics and the Public Service." *Public Administration Review* 24 (December, 1964): 234–43.

Barnds, William J., ed. *The Right to Know, to Withhold and to Lie*. New York: The Council on Religion and International Affairs, 1969.

Barry, Brian. "The Public Interest." *Proceedings of the Aristotelian Society*, supplement. vol. 38, 1964. Reprinted in *The Bias of Pluralism*. Edited by William E. Connolly. New York: Atherton, 1971.

Beard, Edmund and Horn, Stephen. *Congressional Ethics: The View from the House*. Washington, D.C.: The Brookings Institution, 1975.

Beitz, Charles R. "Bounded Morality: Justice and the State in World Politics." *International Organization 33*, no. 3 (Summer 1979).

Bennis, W. "Resigning: A Bureaucrat's Dilemma." In *The Leaning Ivory Tower*. San Francisco, Calif.: Jossey-Bass, 1973.

Bok, Sissela. *Lying: Moral Choice in Public Life*. New York: Pantheon Books, 1978.

Caro, Robert A. *The Power Broker: Robert Moses and the Fall of New York*. New York: Alfred A. Knopf, 1974.

Davis, Kenneth Culp. *Discretionary Justice in Europe and America*. Urbana: University of Illinois Press, 1976.

————. *Discretionary Justice: A Preliminary Inquiry*. Baton Rouge: Louisiana State University Press, 1969.

Dvorin, Eugene and Simmons, Robert H. *From Amoral to Humane Bureaucracy*. New York: Harper & Row, 1972.

Flathman, Richard E. *The Public Interest*. New York: Wiley, 1966.

Friedrich, Carl J. *The Public Interest: Nomos V*. New York: Atherton, 1962.

Fuller, Lon L. *The Morality of Law*. New Haven: Yale University Press, 1964.

Gardiner, John A. and Olson, David J. eds. *Theft of the City: Readings on Corruption in Urban America*. Bloomington, Ind: Indiana University Press, 1974.

Gauthier, David P., ed. *Morality and Rational Self-Interest*. Englewood Cliffs, N.J.: Prentice-Hall, 1970.

Halberstam, David. *The Best and the Brightest*. New York: Random House, 1972.

Harbaugh, William H. *Lawyer's Lawyer: The Life of John W. Davis*. Oxford at the University Press, 1973.

Harmon, Michael M. "Normative Theory and Public Administration: Some Suggestions for a Redefinition of Administrative Responsibility." In *The New Public Administration*. Edited by Frank Marini. Scranton, Pa.: Chandler Publishing Co., 1971.

Held, Virginia. *The Public Interest and Individual Interests*. New York: Basic Books, 1970.

Hirschman, Albert O. *Exit, Voice, and Loyalty: Responses to Decline in Firms, Organizations and States*. Cambridge, Mass.: Harvard University Press, 1970.

Hoopes, Townsend. *The Devil and John Foster Dulles*. Boston, Mass.: Atlantic-Little, Brown, 1973.

Isenberg, Arnold. "Deontology and the Ethics of Lying." In *Ethics*. Edited by Judith J. Thomson and Gerald Dworkin. New York: Harper & Brothers, 1968.

Jowell, Jeffrey L. *Law and Bureaucracy: Administrative Discretion and the Limits of Legal Action*. Port Washington, N.Y.: Dunellen Publishing Co., 1975.

Kadish, Mortimer R. and Kadish, Sanford H. *Discretion to Disobey: A Study of Lawful Departures from Legal Rules*. Stanford, Calif.: Stanford University Press, 1973.

Lowi, Theodore J. *The End of Liberalism: Ideology, Policy, and the Crisis of Public Authority*. New York: W.W. Norton, 1969.

Manchester, William. *American Caesar: Douglas MacArthur 1880–1964*.

Boston: Little, Brown, 1978).

Marini, Frank, ed. *Toward a New Public Administration.* New York: Harper & Row, 1971.

Mason, Alpheus T. *Brandeis: A Free Man's Life.* New York: Viking, 1946.

Morison, Elting E. *Turmoil and Tradition: A Study of the Life and Times of Henry L. Stimson.* New York: Atheneum, 1964.

Mosher, Frederick. *Democracy and the Public Service.* New York: Oxford University Press, 1968.

Nathan, Richard P. *The Plot that Failed.* New York: Wiley, 1975.

Pennock, J. Roland and Chapman, John W. eds. *Political and Legal Obligation: Nomos XII.* New York: Atherton Press, 1970.

Peters, Charles and Branch, Taylor, eds. *Blowing the Whistle: Dissent in the Public Interest.* New York: Praeger, 1972.

Peters, John G. and Welch, Susan. "Political Corruption in America: A Search for Definitions and a Theory, or If Political Corruption is in the Mainstream of American Politics Why is it not in the Mainstream of American Politics Research," *The American Political Science Review* 72, no. 3 (September 1978).

Pitkin, Hanna. *The Concept of Representation.* Berkeley: University of California Press, 1967.

———. *The Politics of a Guaranteed Income.* New York: Vintage, 1973.

Redford, Emmette S. *Democracy in the Administrative State.* New York: Oxford University Press, 1969.

Reisman, W. Michael. *Folded Lies: Bribery, Crusades, and Reform.* New York: The Free Press, 1979.

———, ed. *Representation.* New York: Atherton, 1969.

———, ed. *Responsibility: Nomos III.* New York: The Liberal Arts Press, 1960.

Riemer, Neal. *The Representative: Trustee? Delegate? Partisan? Politico?* Lexington, Mass.: D.C. Heath and Co., 1967.

Rohr, John A. *Ethics and Bureaucrats: An Essay on Law and Values.* New York: Kekker, 1978.

Sherman, Lawrence W. *Scandal and Reform: Controlling Police Corruption.* Berkeley: University of California Press, 1978.

Steiner, Peter O. "The Public Sector and the Public Interest." In *Public Expenditures and Policy Analysis,* Edited by Robert Haveman and Julius Margolis. Chicago: Markham, 1970, pp. 21–58.

Thompson, Dennis F. *The Democratic Citizen: Social Science and Democratic*

Theory in the Twentieth Century. New York: Cambridge University Press, 1970.

Thompson, Victor. *Without Sympathy or Enthusiasm: The Problems of Administrative Compassion*. University, Ala.: University of Alabama Press, 1975.

Thomson, James. "How Could Vietnam Happen?" *Atlantic,* April 1968.

————. "Truth and Politics." In *Between Past and Future*. Baltimore, Md.: Penguin, 1977.

Wakefield, Susan. "Ethics and the Public Service: A Case for Individual Responsibility," *Public Administration Review* 36 (November/December 1976).

Walzer, Michael. *Just and Unjust Wars: A Moral Argument with Historical Illustrations*. New York: Basic Books, 1977.

Walzer, Michael. "Political Action: The Problem of Dirty Hands," *Philosophy and Public Affairs* 2, no. 2 (Winter 1973): 160–80.

Warren, Robert Penn. *All the King's Men*. New York: Random House, 1960.

Weber, Max. "Politics as a Vocation" and "Science as a Vocation." In *From Max Weber,* Edited by H.H. Gerth and C. Wright Mills. New York: Oxford University Press, 1946.

Weisband, Edward and Franck, Thomas M. *Resignation in Protest*. New York: Viking Press, 1975.

Wicker, Tom. *A Time to Die*. New York: New York Times Books, 1975.

Wildavsky, Aaron. "Aesthetic Power or the Triumph of the Sensitive Minority over the Vulgar Mass..." and "A Strategy for Political Participation." In *The Revolt Against the Masses*. New York: Basic Books, 1971.

Wise, David. *The Politics of Lying*. New York: Random House, 1973.

III. Dilemmas of Choice

Aiken, Henry D. "Morality and Ideology." In *Ethics and Society*. Edited by Richard T. De George, Garden City, N.Y.: Doubleday, 1966.

Baier, Kurt. *The Moral Point of View*. New York: Random House, 1966.

Barry, Brian. "Justice Between Generations." In *Law, Morality and Society: Essays in Honour of H. L. A. Hart*. Edited by P. M. S. Hacker and J. Raz. Oxford: Clarendon Press, 1977.

Barry, Brian. *Political Argument*. London: Routledge, 1965.

Beauchamp, Thomas L., ed. *Ethics and Public Policy*. Englewood Cliffs, N.J.: Prentice-Hall, 1975.

Beitz, Charles. "Justice and International Relations," *Philosophy and Public Affairs* (Summer 1975).

Berlin, Isaiah. *Four Essays on Liberty*. Oxford at the University Press, 1969.

Bernstein, Richard J. *The Restructuring of Social and Political Theory*. Philadelphia: University of Pennsylvania Press, 1976.

Brandt, R. B. "Utilitarianism and the Rules of War," *Philosophy and Public Affairs* 1, no. 2 (Winter 1972): 145–65.

Brown, Peter G. and Shue, Henry, eds. *Food Policy: The Responsibility of the United States in the Life and Death Choices*. New York: The Free Press, 1977.

Cohen, Marshall, Nagel, Thomas, and Scanlon, Thomas, eds. *Equality and Preferential Treatment*. Princeton, N.J.: Princeton University Press, 1978.

Daniels, Norman., ed. *Reading Rawls: Critical Studies on Rawls' A Theory of Justice*. New York: Basic Books, 1971.

de Crespigny, Anthony and Wertheimer, Alan, eds. *Contemporary Political Theory*. New York: Atherton Press, 1970.

Dworkin, Ronald. *Taking Rights Seriously*. Cambridge, Mass.: Harvard University Press, 1978.

Feiveson, Harold A., Sinden, Frank W., and Socolow, Robert H. eds. *Boundaries of Analysis: An Inquiry into the Tocks Island Dam Controversy*. Cambridge, Mass.: Ballinger, 1976.

Flathman, Richard E. *Concepts in Social and Political Philosophy*. New York: Macmillan, 1973.

Frankena, William K. *Ethics*. Englewood Cliffs, N.J.: Prentice-Hall, 1963.

Hampshire, Stuart, ed. *Public and Private Morality*. New York: Cambridge University Press, 1978.

Hart, H. L. A. *The Concept of Law*. New York: Cambridge University Press, 1961.

Keynes, John Maynard. "My Early Beliefs." In *Two Memoirs*. New York: Kelley, 1949.

Leys, Wayne A. R. *Ethics for Policy Decisions: The Art of Asking Deliberative Questions*. New York: Prentice-Hall, Inc., 1952.

———. *The Liberal Theory of Justice*. Oxford: Clarendon Press, 1973.

Macpherson, C. B. *Democratic Theory: Essays in Retrieval*. Oxford: Clarendon Press, 1973.

McWilliams, Wilson Carey. *The Idea of Fraternity in America*. Berkeley: University of California Press, 1973.

Melden, Abraham Irving, ed. *Human Rights*. Belmont, Calif.: Wadsworth, 1970.

Mosher, Frederick. *Watergate: Implications for Responsible Government*. New York: Basic Books, 1974.

———. "New Reflections on Ethics and Foreign Policy: The Problem of Human Rights," *Journal of Politics* 40, no. 1 (November 1978): 984–1010.

Niebuhr, Reinhold. *Moral Man and Immoral Society*. New York: Charles Scribner's Sons, 1932.

Passmore, John. *Man's Responsibility for Nature*. New York: Charles Scribner's Sons, 1974.

Pennock, J. Roland and Chapman, John, eds. *Equality: Nomos IX*. New York: Atherton, 1967.

Pitkin, Hanna Fenichel. *Wittgenstein and Justice: On the Significance of Ludwig Wittgenstein for Social and Political Thought*. Berkeley: University of California Press, 1972.

Rawls, John. *A Theory of Justice*. Cambridge, Mass.: Harvard University Press, 1972.

Schaar, John M. "Equality of Opportunity and Beyond." In *Contemporary Political Theory*. Edited by Anthony de Crespigny and Alan Wertheimer. Chicago: Aldine, 1970.

Sikora, R. I. and Brian Barry, eds. *Obligations to Future Generations*. Philadelphia, Pa.: Temple University Press, 1978.

Smart, J. J. C. and Bernard Williams. *Utilitarianism For and Against*. Cambridge at the University Press, 1973.

Stanley, John. "Equality of Opportunity as Philosophy and Ideology," *Political Theory* 5, no. 1 (February 1977): 61–74.

Stone, Christopher. *Do Trees Have Standing?* Las Altos: W. Kaufman, 1974.

Thompson, Kenneth W. "Moral Reasoning in American Thought on War and Peace," *The Review of Politics* 39, no. 3 (July 1977).

Tribe, Laurence H. *When Values Conflict: Essays on Environmental Analysis, Discourse and Decision*. Cambridge, Mass.: Ballinger, 1976.

Varian, Hal R. "Distributive Justice, Welfare Economics and the Theory of Fairness," *Philosophy and Public Policy* (Spring 1975).

Walzer, Michael. *Just and Unjust Wars*. New York: Basic Books, 1977.

Wasserstrom, Richard A. *Morality and the Law*. Belmont, Calif.: Wadsworth

Publishing Co., 1971.

Williams, Bernard. "The Idea of Equality." In *Philosophy, Politics and Society, Second Series*. Edited by Peter Laslett and W. F. Runciman. Oxford: Blackwell, 1972, pp. 110–31.

Williams, Bernard, *Morality: An Introduction to Ethics*. New York: Harper & Row, 1972.

Wolff, Robert Paul. *Understanding Rawls: A Reconstruction and Critique of A Theory of Justice*. Princeton, N.Y.: Princeton University Press, 1977.

Wolin, Sheldon. "Political Theory as a Vocation," *American Political Science Review* 63, no. 4 (December 1969).

Publications from The Teaching of Ethics Project
The Hastings Center

A number of publications on the teaching of ethics in higher education are available from The Hastings Center. A list of these publications appears on the back cover. Return order form to: The Hastings Center, 360 Broadway, Hastings-on-Hudson, N.Y. 10706

I. **The Teaching of Ethics in Higher Education: A Report by The Hastings Center** · · · · · · · · · · ($5) _____

II. Michael J. Kelly, Legal Ethics and Legal Education · · · · · · · · · · · · · · · · · · ($4) _____

III. Clifford G. Christians & Catherine L. Covert, **Teaching Ethics in Journalism Education** · · · · · ($4) _____

IV. K. Danner Clouser, **Teaching Bioethics: Strategies, Problems, and Resources** · · · · · · · · · ($4) _____

V. Charles W. Powers & David Vogel, **Ethics in the Education of Business Managers.** · · · · · · · · ($5) _____

VI. Donald P. Warwick, **The Teaching of Ethics in the Social Sciences.** · · · · · · · · · · · · ($4) _____

VII. Robert J. Baum, **Ethics and Engineering Curricula.** · · · · · · · · · · · · · · · · ($4) _____

VIII. Joel L. Fleishman & Bruce L. Payne, **Ethical Dilemmas and the Education of Policymakers** · · · · ($4) _____

IX. Bernard Rosen & Arthur C. Caplan, **Ethics in the Undergraduate Curriculum.** · · · · · · · · · ($4) _____

TOTAL COST _____

PRICES QUOTED ARE POSTPAID—
PREPAYMENT IS REQUIRED
There will be a $1 service charge
if billing is necessary.

Name _____

Address _____

City _____ State _____ Zip Code _____